PRAISE FOR
ATTRACT & GROW

"I owe everything to David Scranton. He's allowed me to go from being a business operator to a business owner. Clients and prospects can see that. They can perceive when they're working with an advisor who is a notch above."

– Matt J.

"Through Dave, I've grown not only professionally but personally. His focus on truly helping clients, and making that the foundation that you build upon, changed everything for me. My job became my passion, and success grew naturally from there."

– Michael E.

"I was just another advisor out there chasing prospects with the same old products and strategies every other advisor was using. With Dave, I learned how to differentiate myself and stand out from the pack. I learned how to attract clients instead of chasing them, and my business took off!"

– Anthony S.

"There aren't many true visionaries in our industry, but David Scranton is one of them. His vision has helped me not only grow my business but improve my life and the lives of all my clients. That's what real leadership can do."

– Jeff S.

ATTRACT & GROW

DAVID J. SCRANTON

ATTRACT & GROW

THE FINANCIAL ADVISOR'S
BLUEPRINT FOR ATTRACTING
$50 MILLION IN ANNUAL ASSETS

 Advantage | Books

Published by Advantage Books, Charleston, South Carolina.
An imprint of Advantage Media.

ADVANTAGE is a registered trademark, and the Advantage colophon is a trademark of Advantage Media Group, Inc.

Printed in the United States of America.

10 9 8 7 6 5 4 3 2 1

ISBN: 979-8-89188-097-9 (Paperback)
ISBN: 979-8-89188-098-6 (eBook)

Library of Congress Control Number: 2024922830

Cover design by Lance Buckley.
Layout design by Ruthie Wood.

This publication is designed to provide accurate and authoritative information in regard to the subject matter covered. It is sold with the understanding that the publisher is not engaged in rendering legal, accounting, or other professional services. If legal advice or other expert assistance is required, the services of a competent professional person should be sought.

Investment Advisory Services offered through Sound Income Strategies, LLC, an SEC Registered Investment Advisory Firm. Sound Income Group, Sound Income Academy, Retirement Income Source®, and Sound Income Strategies, LLC are associated entities.

Chapter 7 is based on the copyrighted material of Sandler and Mattson Enterprise, Inc.: 5 Stages of Entrepreneurial Growth©

Advantage Books is an imprint of Advantage Media Group. Advantage Media helps busy entrepreneurs, CEOs, and leaders write and publish a book to grow their business and become the authority in their field. Advantage authors comprise an exclusive community of industry professionals, idea-makers, and thought leaders. For more information go to **advantagemedia.com**.

This book I dedicate to my late mother. From her I learned that the keys to overcoming any challenge life throws at you are stubborn persistence and a tireless work ethic. For her, those traits were a product of her Polish heritage. For me, they provided life lessons that helped me persevere through years of pushback and adversity early in my career. So, thank you, Mom, for making me the "stubborn Pollock" I needed to be to stick with it and make my dreams come true. I owe it all to you!

CONTENTS

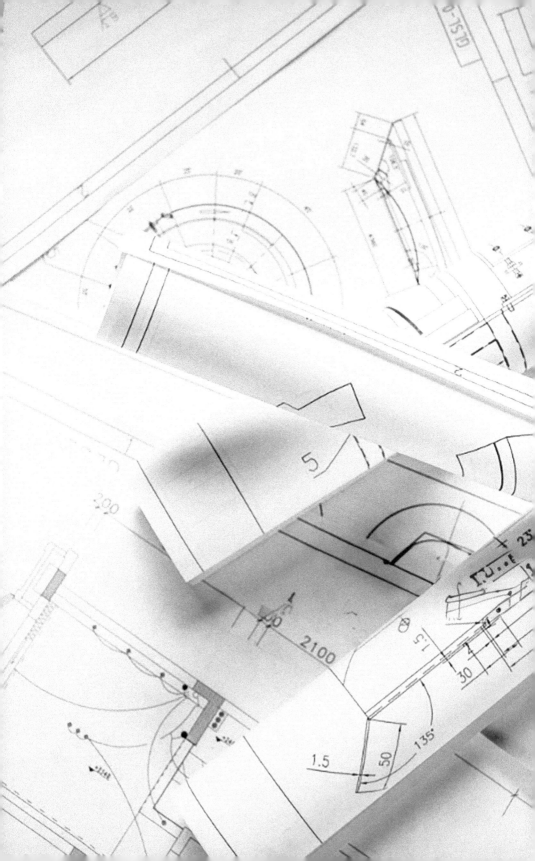

INTRODUCTION

I'm not for long introductions, and I like to get straight to the point.

Chances are, if you're reading this book, you're a financial advisor who falls into one of three categories. First, maybe you're someone who is struggling. You're questioning why you're even in this industry and thinking it's time to move on to something different.

Second, maybe you love what you do and have seen a base level of success, but you feel stuck. No matter what you do, you feel trapped in this endless cycle of chasing clients—only to see most of them run in fear. You keep thinking, *Is there something about my personality that is off? Why do I spend most of my time chasing when I've got such a great service everyone should want?*

Or third, you're already a top advisor but eager to grow your business and build a *team* of advisors you oversee. However, you fear delegation and releasing control of the empire you've built. You fear that by bringing on other advisors, you'll be training your future competitors. As a result, you've settled for being a great advisor, but you're unable to scale to where you want to go.

Regardless of your category, I am confident this book will steer you in the right direction. As someone who started with nothing, almost gave up, and now mentors dozens of advisors each year and manages over $3 billion in assets, I know each category I've outlined above very well and what it takes to move on to the next stage.

Every advisor is different. Maybe you want to earn a decent living and provide a solid service for your clients. Great! Or perhaps you're a tad more ambitious and want to develop a team. That's also great. This book isn't designed to tell you which category you should be in. It's designed to help you create clear goals, develop a clear blueprint for success, and provide the skills necessary to grow your organization as large as you would like.

With that said, let's get started.

PART I:
The AIDA Strategy

CHAPTER 1

HOW PROSPECTS BECOME CLIENTS

Why am I working so hard and not seeing meaningful results?

This was the question I kept asking myself for nine long years. After earning my undergraduate math degree in 1987, I was full of testosterone and eager to tackle the world. Still in my twenties, I didn't mind chasing prospects and thrived on cold-calling. But it didn't take me long to figure out I had a problem.

Despite my efforts, I couldn't break the $100,000 in gross income barrier. Even in the '90s, when incomes were lower, I knew I had a problem and felt embarrassed by my lack of success. It wasn't like I had a bad life, but I knew I wasn't living up to my potential and couldn't figure out why. Thinking education was the answer to my problems, I earned every degree I could—CLU, CHFC, CFP, MSFS, CFA, you name it. But nothing changed.

At first, I took pride in my effort and a sense of sick pleasure from plowing my way through rejection. But finally, after nine exhausting years, I reached the point where I'd had enough. I was sick of attending large financial planning conferences and noticing many of my peers were bringing in triple my earnings with half the stress. While I had to scratch and claw to turn prospects into clients, my competitors seemed to do this with ease. They were selling; I was not.

This forced me to ask myself a tough question: *What do they have that I don't?* My fear of burnout and search for answers placed me on a lifelong mission and brought me to this simple yet profound realization: the most successful producers in the financial services industry don't chase; they attract.

From Struggles to Success

By 1995, my discouragement had reached a point where I started looking for a way out and applying to medical schools. Not wanting to leave the financial services industry on a low note, I resolved to give it one more shot and set a goal to earn $125,000 in 1996. In my mind, achieving this milestone would validate my success and pave the way for pursuing medical school. With determination, guidance from a mentor, and relentless effort, I worked hard and surpassed my goal by $2,000, earning a cool $127,000 that year.

Suddenly, the prospect of medical school lost its allure, and I resolved to do even better the following year and set a goal to earn $175,000. Still, on January 1, 1997, I was plagued with doubt. *Could I replicate my success? Was last year merely a stroke of luck?* In 365 days, I had my answer. Once again, I'd exceeded my expectations and hit $183,000 in gross income. After years of disappointment in setting goals and falling short, for two consecutive years, I'd been successful, which instilled a newfound confidence in my ability to achieve. By 1999, I had broken the $300,000 mark and decided to seek guidance from a new mentor.

That's when my career really skyrocketed, and six years later, my company made over $3 million in revenue.

In 2006, I established a field marketing organization (FMO) called Advisors' Academy. Our value proposition was that if advisors committed to putting all their fixed and indexed annuity businesses through our FMO, we would, in turn, teach them how to manage money for their clients and how to market and generate leads for themselves. We'd also teach them to become better salespeople and how to manage their practices as independent advisors.

As you can imagine, because we were asking for a little while giving a lot, this business took off. A few years later, our advisors came to us and said, "We appreciate your generosity in everything you've done, but we don't want to manage money anymore. We want to be asset gatherers." So in 2014, we started Sound Income Strategies to be able to take that money management function off the plates of our independent advisors. My goal wasn't to make more money. I simply noticed a need and wanted to do something about it.

In 2019, I realized that because of our coaching, all our advisors were marketing in the same way, presenting solutions to prospects in the same way, and running their practices in the same way. As a result, their clients' money was being managed in the same way. I also realized that whenever one of our advisors spoke about our unique selling proposition to a client, the client immediately grasped what they were saying and responded with statements like, "Wow, this makes so much sense. Why aren't *other* advisors doing this?" Realizing we would be stronger if we all could market under one brand to give consumers the confidence of quality control, we started a national franchise known as the Retirement Income Source®.

That's the success part of the story. But you're probably thinking, *David, this all sounds wonderful, but I feel like you're leaving out a few details. How did you jump from being ready to leave the industry to the success you experience today?*

Part of this growth came from a change in strategy. For example, in 1999, noticing a drop in the stock market was coming, I shifted from a *growth-based* model of investing to an *income-generating* model. Hard work was also a factor. However, I attribute most of my success to a proven strategy called AIDA, which stands for Attention, Interest, Desire, and Action.

The AIDA model originated in 1898, when American advertising advocate and pioneer Elias St. Elmo Lewis proposed it in a magazine article.[1] It's a road map for understanding how advertising grabs our attention, sparks our interest, creates desire, and leads to action. Ever since Lewis came up with it, the AIDA model has been a cornerstone of marketing and advertising strategies, and I've since refined its application for financial advisors.

Since 2006, I've used this tool to coach hundreds of different advisors on how to stop chasing and start attracting prospects. All four stages are pivotal. Mess up on any of them, and your prospects will run. Do these steps well, and you'll be shocked at the prospects you attract.

Stop Chasing, Start Attracting

Intuitively, the whole attract versus chase approach makes sense.

Let's say you're going for a nice evening stroll in your community. Suddenly, a random stranger starts walking behind you. Not giving

---

1   "Aida (Marketing)," Wikipedia, September 27, 2024, https://en.wikipedia.org/wiki/AIDA_(marketing).

it much thought, you turn the next corner. The stranger turns. You walk up Main Street. The stranger follows. You veer down an alley, and he's hot on your heels. Feeling a bit intimidated, you break into a sprint and glance over your shoulder to see this mysterious man is matching your every stride.

Now you're really spooked and looking for any opportunity to escape. Then something unexpected happens. After several blocks, you give a quick look and notice the stranger has stopped chasing you and is casually walking in the opposite direction. Picturing yourself in one of those Choose Your Own Adventure books, what decision would you make next?

If you're like 99.9 percent of rational individuals, you will get as far away from this stranger as possible, find a safe path home, and possibly call the authorities. The one thing you *won't* do is turn around and try to find him. Why? Because it's almost impossible to get somebody who has just been *chased* and turn them into a *chaser*.

The Key to Attraction

The same principle holds true in the financial services industry. Whenever you start chasing customers, they run. And even when you stop, they'll want nothing to do with you because they're spooked. But when you learn the art of attraction, you become the one they pursue. This is why the AIDA formula is so important. By paying attention to each step, you shift from *chasing* to *attracting*.

ATTENTION: DIFFERENTIATION

In the financial services industry, you generate *attention* by having a business model that differentiates you from your competitors. Blending in with the masses is the enemy of attention and relegates you to a life of chasing. For example, take a look at the picture below of a team of advisors. Can you figure out which one stands out from the crowd? I'll give you a hint. It's the only one in a blue suit! This is how you generate attention. But differentiating yourself and generating attention is not enough.

Most prospects come to us with their guards up. They don't want to get sold. They may think they have a little bit of a problem but underestimate its significance. At this point, what you do next will determine if you convert them into a client or if they dash for the door. To generate attention, you must have a business model that differentiates you from your competitors. You need to stand out. Otherwise, you'll be relegated to a life of chasing.

INTEREST: BRANDING

The *interest* part is branding. People need to know who you are and what you do. Think of branding as education. You also need to position yourself in such a way that creates *interest* with others and brands you with your business model. Unfortunately, in the financial services industry, we usually don't have the patience for branding efforts to pay off. Instead, all we think about is lead generation. However, this is a mistake because long-term solid brand interest is more important than short-term sales. The first is a sustainable model; the second is not. Branding makes you seem like a safer option when compared to your competitors. It increases your lead generation efforts, makes you more effective, and helps increase your closing ratios.

DESIRE: LEAD GENERATION

After you've gained your customers' attention and built interest in your brand, you've got to transition them from interest to *desire*. Desire is about lead generation. In the financial services world, desire has to do with having a lead generation system that allows you to attract and not chase. Some lead generation systems are chasing-based, and some are attraction-based. The more you can do the attraction type, the less you spook your prospects. Lead generation is what helps you go from interest to desire.

This is where your customers raise their hands and want to talk with you about what you could do for them. How do you do this? By offering free dinner seminars at Ruth's Chris Steak House? Not exactly. While marketing like this can work, I think this can often send the wrong message. Let's face it. If the only way you can get prospects to hear you speak is by having them eat a steak dinner, you're chasing them. You know it, and your prospects know it. Again, that's not to say dinner seminars can't work, but they introduce an additional challenge in getting people to become chasers. A better approach is to generate leads with attraction-based systems.

ACTION: SALES PROCESS

Then you've positioned yourself for the last step in the AIDA process—*action*. This is where many advisors spook their prospects, causing them to run. Why? Because most sales processes in the financial services industry are either never taught or are chasing-based. And because advisors don't have a consistent attraction-based sales process that helps them turn potential clients from desire to action, everything fizzles out.

Keep in mind this is where a lot of financial planners go wrong. When they go to close, they pounce on people or use cringy sales tactics that give off a bad vibe and spook their prospects. But that's not what you will do, not after reading this book. When you have a clear sales process in place, prospects now understand how you want them to take action.

This is why it's imperative to have a low-key, attraction-based sales process. One where you're not trying to strong-arm prospects into making a decision, but you're helping them discover they've got a problem and that you can provide the solution. It's a slow and methodical process rather than a quick and easy pitch.

The whole premise of the AIDA formula is that when people start to move toward you, they come *slowly*, as they're only somewhat attracted. Then that attraction builds into an interest in learning more about you. Eventually, that interest turns into a desire to talk to you, and that desire turns into action, whereby they become clients or customers.

From your vantage point, you draw *attention* to your product or service, generate *interest* in your brand, stimulate a *desire* for what you're offering, and spur *action* to try or buy. From your prospect's perspective, they're shifting from *What is this?* to *I like this* to *I want this* to *I'm getting this!*

Attraction in Action

If you've ever gone fishing for something like white marlin or sailfish, you know this process can be a bit finicky, and there are strong parallels between attracting *fish* and attracting *prospects*. Attracting fish hundreds of feet below the water's surface is no easy feat and requires meticulous persistence.

It starts with having a boat that looks right, sounds right, and generates the right *attention*. Some boats have a funny vibration that repels fish, and those boats don't work. But other boats are perfect for generating attention and raising fish to the surface. At this point, the fish are curious but will usually keep their distance and remain several hundred feet behind your boat.

After you've generated attention, it's time to create some *interest* and get them closer to the boat. To do this, you might put some teasers, or lures without hooks, in the water and drag these behind. These increase the fish's interest, and they start to swim closer to the boat, hoping these teasers are a school of bait fish.

From here, you want to turn that interest into *desire*. You gradually start to pull the teasers away, and when that happens, your fish start to chase the teaser. If they are hungry, you might have to speed up the process. Then, when they're just about ready to bite, you pull the teaser out of the water, causing the fish to want what they can't have.

Now is the time for *action*. You've got to put actual bait in the water with an actual hook. And you've got to put the line and bait in the right place, where you think the fish will bite. Then, when you see the fish getting ready to make their move, you dump the rod tip and put it in free spool. You disengage the reel's drag or tension mechanism, allowing the line to run freely off the reel without resistance so the fish can actually eat the bait. Then you wait for the appropriate time, push up the drag, and boom! You've caught yourself a fish.

While this process might sound easy, it requires a lot of careful work and attention to detail. The teasers must be placed in the right spot behind the boat, and the boat's got to be trolling at just the right speed to make the teasers look like realistic bait fish. Then you must pull the teasers out at the exact right pace and be prepared for when the fish strikes. Mess up on any of these steps, and the fish will be spooked—never to be seen again.

Even if you get three out of four steps right, that's still not enough. You've got to nail every single one. The same is true with prospects.

Become an Attractive Person

In John Maxwell's *The 21 Irrefutable Laws of Leadership*, he shares what he calls the Law of Magnetism. "Who you are is who you attract."[2] This means if you're constantly negative and pessimistic, there is a good chance you'll attract negative and pessimistic friends, employees, and clients.

If you've always operated with a chase mindset, you'll probably need to rethink how you present yourself to others. It's the little things like how you walk into a room, look someone in the eye, or follow up after an initial consultation. It's shifting from being an obnoxious salesperson that prospects avoid to becoming an attractive person others trust and want to follow.

In sales, I often use that familiar saying "No one cares how much you know until they know how much you care." To truly excel in the financial services industry, you must care about your prospects.

---

2   John C. Maxwell, *The 21 Irrefutable Laws of Leadership* (Nashville: Thomas Nelson, 2007).

This may come naturally when you're already successful, but it's a lot tougher to practice when living paycheck to paycheck. When you're desperate, prospects pick up on this immediately and are repulsed. This was my problem for the first nine years I was an advisor.

But when you're calm, caring, and competent, you become the advisor prospects can't resist.

CHAPTER 2

WHY DIFFERENTIATION IS THE KEY TO GENERATING ATTENTION

A*IDA*

So how do you generate attention?

Determining an effective business model that sets you apart from your competitors is crucial, and differentiation is powerful for two reasons. First, it helps you stand out by grabbing a prospect's attention. It's the shiny boat in the water that stimulates the fish's curiosity. Second, differentiation plays into the prospect's increasing desire for *specialists* over *generalists*. Specialists, like in the legal or medical fields, tend to earn more and serve their clients more effectively.

Picture this hypothetical scenario. Let's say you move to a new community and have two options. Option A is selling a product everyone wants but pits you against a hundred other sellers. Option B is to offer a product that only appeals to 10 percent of the population but makes you the sole provider in your area. Which option would you choose?

If you're like 99.9 percent of the advisors who participate in my training sessions, you choose option B. This philosophy is the central premise of *Blue Ocean Strategy*, authored by W. Chan Kim and Renée Mauborgne. This book discusses two distinct business environments: a "red ocean" and a "blue ocean." In a red ocean, you're part of a fiercely competitive market where businesses struggle for market share. You might gain some ground, but dominating the market is unlikely. A blue ocean, on the other hand, is where you find yourself without any real competition.

You're creating a valuable service no one else is offering. As the authors share, "Value innovation is the cornerstone of blue ocean strategy. We call it value innovation because instead of focusing on beating the competition, you focus on making the competition irrelevant by creating a leap in value for buyers and your company, thereby opening up new and uncontested market space."[3]

The key to adopting a blue ocean strategy and generating attention in the financial services industry is differentiation.

Find Your Niche

The way you differentiate yourself from the competition is by finding your niche.

It's falling into what I call the "Goldilocks Zone"—not too broad, not too narrow. Being too broad makes you a generalist, while being too narrow risks falling prey to the "Susan Lucci effect." For younger readers, Susan Lucci is a well-known actress who became famous for her role as Erica Kane on the soap opera *All My Children*, a part she played for more than four decades. Despite her success and popularity in this role, Lucci became so identified with her character and the

---

3   W. Chan Kim and Renée Mauborgne, *Blue Ocean Strategy, Expanded Edition: How to Create Uncontested Market Space and Make the Competition Irrelevant* (Boston: Harvard Business Review Press, 2015).

world of daytime television that it was challenging for her to find opportunities in prime-time television shows and movies.

Financial advisors face a similar challenge. In some industries, you can be known for a specific product or service, such as annuities, but this can become limiting if influential voices in the market speak against your niche. In a large metropolitan area, a narrow specialization might work due to the large population, but generally, a niche that's too specific may not be sustainable.

It's also important to consider what *doesn't* constitute a specialty. Many advisors might claim superior client service as their differentiator. Still, since this isn't a tangible specialty, and *every* competitor claims good service, it doesn't serve as an effective differentiator to prospects. Some advisors may claim knowledge in areas like Social Security, and yes, that *was* an area of specialty at one time. The problem today is that so many financial advisors are conducting seminars for Social Security and claiming to be experts that it's no longer a blue ocean strategy. Even if you're among the few with high certifications as a social security expert, it's hard to differentiate yourself.

What *does* constitute a specialty? There are various examples I could list. For instance, in our organization, we have advisors who hold specialized designations, and they work with clients who fit within those specializations. We also have others who specialize in special needs planning, whether it be for children or parents. They are performing unique services for specific situations. These are just two examples of advisors who, through their specialties, are not allowing prospects to commoditize them.

The sweet spot is the Goldilocks Zone—not too broad or too narrow. Ultimately, the goal is to find a niche that not only distinguishes you from the competition but aligns with your passion. Your business model should enable you to thrive in your chosen niche rather than serve as a means to an end. When you discover your niche, you differentiate yourself from the competition, and others can't help but take notice.

This was my story.

Specializing in Income Generating Strategies

I grew up in Bristol, Connecticut, before ESPN moved into town and put our community on the map. My mom worked in a factory, and my dad worked in construction. When I entered the financial services industry, I initially targeted business owners and affluent individuals, as I was advised that this was where the most significant financial opportunities lay. However, I soon discovered my true passion was assisting the average mom-and-pop investor.

From my viewpoint, if someone had $20 million in assets, they'd have to screw up badly to be eating cat food in retirement. On the other hand, I realized many had never earned six figures annually but had diligently accumulated between one and two million in their 401(k) plans. It was these individuals, with more modest savings, who genuinely needed guidance.

> When you discover your niche, you differentiate yourself from the competition, and others can't help but take notice.

They were what authors Thomas J. Stanley and William D. Danko would call *The Millionaire Next Door*. They had budgeted carefully, invested wisely, and prioritized financial independence over social status. That said, while they had done well for themselves, they couldn't afford to be reckless with their money.

These were the people I determined to help, but there was a problem. In 1999, with my focus on the stock market, I grew concerned as price-earnings ratios across the S&P 500 approached forty. I knew the market was going to drop. And I also knew from my studies of stock market history that it would take a while to recover when it dropped.

As a CFA, my training taught me that I could build bond ladders or buy preferred stock if I wanted to protect people from stock market losses. But I knew building bond ladders as a broker was not a sustainable business model; I realized I was at a crossroads. I didn't want to lay off my assistant, but it looked like I had no other options. I felt I needed to pull my clients out of the market, but I also knew nobody wanted to work with a broke financial advisor. I didn't know what to do.

That's when I was introduced to fixed and indexed annuities, and this became a turning point for me. I could still put a majority of their money in bonds and bond-like instruments, but incorporating even a modest allocation of clients' portfolios into annuities allowed me to maintain my operations—keeping my assistant employed and the office running. I realized I could protect my clients from the impending drop *and* make a great living.

Word soon spread in the community that if investors wanted *growth*, they could go to companies like Shearson Lehman or A. G. Edwards—both no longer in existence today. But if they wanted *income*, they should go see Dave Scranton because I'd developed a reputation as the guy specializing in, as I called it, "the universe of income-generating strategies." It's no coincidence that this was the six-year time frame in which the annual revenue in my company increased from $300,000 to $3 million.

I'd finally discovered my attention-getter, my point of differentiation, my niche.

TR = I + G

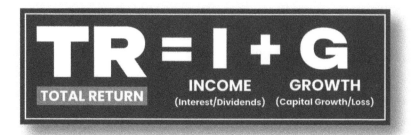

Now you might be reading this today and thinking, *Gee, Dave, that's a compelling story, but that was a quarter of a century ago. How can this help me today?*

Start by asking yourself: *Is there someone in my community who has successfully branded themselves as the go-to expert of income-generating strategies?* I'm not referring to someone on the radio who claims to specialize in income strategies but only sells annuities. I mean someone who truly encompasses the universe of income-generating strategies.

Unless one of our advisors is in your vicinity, the likelihood is that you don't have such a competitor. So astonishingly, a quarter-century later, this philosophy remains a blue ocean strategy that you can adopt as a financial advisor to distinguish yourself from your competitors.

At our companies, we teach financial advisors to utilize annuities for a portion of people's retirement assets. Still, most of our work involves using individual securities for our clients' benefit. We try to avoid mutual funds with their additional layers of fees, which give clients the impression that their advisors aren't doing much beyond selecting some funds. Instead, we manage individual bond portfolios and the portfolios of individual preferred stocks. We integrate business development companies (BDCs), real estate investment trusts (REITs), and high-dividend common stocks. In essence, we're bringing actively managed, institutional-style money management to the average investor with a primary focus on income.

At every seminar, workshop, and meeting, I always underscore a simple yet powerful equation to attendees: total return (TR) is the sum of income (I) and growth (G), or TR = I + G. While this sounds simple, you'd be surprised how many clients do not understand it and conflate income and growth.

I routinely ask people how much income, interest, or dividends their portfolio generates, and they respond with something like, "Well, last year, it did 15 percent," when they're quoting their total return. So I educate people that in their accumulation years, they want to focus on total return and that it doesn't matter whether it comes from income or growth.

> We're bringing actively managed, institutional-style money management to the average investor with a primary focus on income.

But as they're within approximately ten years of retirement, those transition years, they should no longer be ambivalent. Suddenly, the source is important. And for many people who've done a good job saving, income takes priority over growth. It doesn't mean that they can't get growth; it just means that an income-first and growth-second approach is more prudent at this stage.

Where Advisors Go Wrong

Unfortunately, most financial advisors do not generate income the right way. They engineer income by attempting to convert capital gains to income through systematic withdrawals. Often this is done by quoting the 4 percent rule. The main reason is they don't have the bandwidth to invest for income the way we do. It could be knowledge, staffing, or limited financial bandwidth. Let me explain the magnitude of the problem.

For years, a famous mutual fund family advertised their mixed portfolios, claiming an 85 percent success rate with their investment strategies. Every time I saw these promotions, I went nuts, knowing that if the advisors who sold these funds had an honest conversation with their prospects, not one of them would choose to move forward with their company.

Similarly, in 2023, a Morningstar study estimated "that retirees drawing down income from an investment portfolio can now afford to withdraw as much as 4.0% as an initial spending rate, assuming a 90% probability of still having funds remaining after a 30-year time horizon."[4] This approach was supported by Monte Carlo simulations, estimating a success probability based on not depleting your funds before death. While the tone of this article sounds optimistic, it didn't diminish the reality that there was a staggering 10 percent chance of failure. In theory, this is not a big deal because 85 to 90 percent still sounds like a significant number. But when you sit down with a prospect and have a clear conversation with them, you realize how terrible this approach is. For example, imagine saying to a potential client, "I would love for you to invest with me. But know there's a 10 or 15 percent chance you could deplete your funds and be ruined financially. With that out of the way, here is the paperwork. Sign here. There are three copies, so press hard!"

I guarantee you nearly every prospect would run for the door. Unfortunately, we're not as blunt as we should be in our business. We

---

4   Amy C. Arnott, "The Good News on Safe Withdrawal Rates," Morning-star, November 13, 2023, https://www.morningstar.com/retirement/good-news-safe-withdrawal-rates.

don't talk about what can go wrong. Instead, we talk about the glass half full and are not as honest and forthcoming as necessary.

As someone who is an airline-transport-rated pilot and flight instructor, let's say you got in my airplane, and the moment you boarded, I said, "Good evening, ladies and gentlemen, welcome aboard Dave Scranton Airlines. We are ten minutes ahead of schedule, and the current temperature is a balmy eighty-two degrees. We hope you enjoy your flight and are pleased to announce you have a 90 percent chance of arriving alive!" Chances are, after hearing this announcement, you're looking for a new pilot because the risks are just too great.

Imagine what would happen with your client's retirement money in the first thirteen years of retirement if they retire in January 1, 2000:

INVESTMENT PERFORMANCE SIMULATION

What if your client invested $2,000,000 in the S&P 500, beginning in 2000, with an $80,000 annual withdrawal?

Year	Annual Return	Annual Withdrawal	Beginning of Year Value	End of Year Value
2000	-9.10%	-$80,000	$2,000,000	$1,725,355.76
2001	-11.89%	-$80,000	$1,725,355.76	$1,427,129.10
2002	-22.10%	-$80,000	$1,427,129.1	$1,028,458.67
2003	28.67%	-$80,000	$1,028,458.67	$1,217,205.20
2004	10.88%	-$80,000	$1,217,205.2	$1,250,353.61
2005	4.91%	-$80,000	$1,250,353.61	$1,215,652.43
2006	15.78%	-$80,000	$1,215,652.43	$1,306,943.93
2007	5.57%	-$80,000	$1,306,943.93	$1,286,149.64
2008	-37.00%	-$80,000	$1,286,149.64	$740,826.95
2009	26.45%	-$80,000	$740,826.95	$831,344.42
2010	15.06%	-$80,000	$831,344,.42	$857,384.94
2011	2.11%	-$80,000	$857,384.94	$787,607.03
2012	15.99%	-$80,000	$787,607.03	$821,634.00

Source: S&P 500   *assuming 1% management fee

As financial advisors, we owe it to our clients to be brutally honest. The problem is we often worry that this type of brutal honesty can repel potential clients. And perhaps it can. The good news is there *is* an alternative where you can be brutally honest because the bad news isn't really that bad.

Three Things Every Prospect Wants

For your clients who are retired or approaching retirement, most often, the way to look out for your clients' best interests is by helping them develop income-based strategies. This is the main reason many of the financial advisors I mentor consistently bring in between $50 million and $100 million of new assets every year. Using this approach, they feel like they have a bazooka in their briefcase—a secret of which their competitors are unaware.

Think about which prospects can benefit from investing for income in their portfolios. There are three categories of prospects: those who want to increase their income, diminish their risk, and boost their returns.

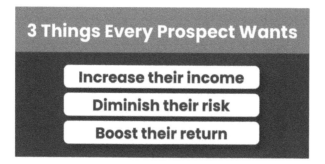

The first category is obvious. *Everyone* near or at the retirement stage of life wants more income. The second is trickier, but there are practical ways to diminish risk. High-dividend stocks are generally less volatile than growth stocks, while bonds typically exhibit even less volatility than all stocks. Many annuities, in turn, are less volatile than bonds, meaning that income-oriented investments can reduce overall volatility and risk.

What is often overlooked is that income can also enhance one's returns. From 1930 to 2021, dividend income made up 40% of the total return of the S&P 500® index.[5] Considering the stock market averages returns of 10 to 11 percent over time, one might incorrectly assume that the average market dividend yield is around 4 to 4.5 percent, but this is not the case. The current dividend on the S&P index is a third of that.

These academic studies always seem to stop short of explaining why those dividends are so important. Years ago, I set out to discover why. I determined that it lies in the concept of dollar-cost averaging, which dividends facilitate in the stock market. Ignoring taxes for the moment, if the market were to rise consistently without fluctuation, dividends and growth would contribute equally to wealth accumulation. However, the market is known for its volatility and doesn't increase in a straight line. During downturns, dividends become more advantageous because they enable the purchase of additional shares at lower prices.

Consider the period from 2000 to 2012, a full thirteen years where the market was volatile and typically lower than where it started. During those years, the market incurred nearly a 50 percent loss when the tech bubble burst, recovering momentarily in 2007. It then experienced a greater than 50 percent drop when the financial crisis hit in 2008, finally recovering by the end of 2012. If you had invested solely in growth stocks during this time,

---

5   Fidelity Investments, "Inflation and Dividend Stocks," Fidelity, accessed March 8, 2024, https://www.fidelity.com/learning-center/smart-money/trading-vs-investing.

you would have seen no gains after thirteen years. However, with a consistent 4 percent dividend reinvested annually, you would have acquired 52 percent more shares by the end of the same period simply from reinvestment. And because you would have been buying more shares when prices were low, the actual increase in share ownership could have been as high as 70 to 80 percent. Consequently, while growth investors were breaking even, you could have been up by 70 to 80 percent due to the additional shares acquired through dividends.

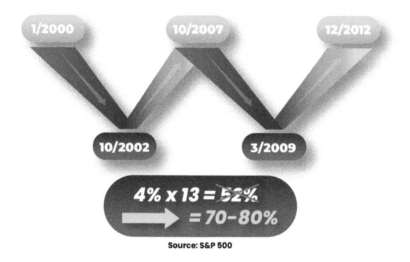

Source: S&P 500

This third category surprises many advisors, even though it shouldn't. Think for a moment about how we're taught to generate more returns for clients. If you've studied the same things I did, the answer would be to "take more risks." However, while that's one way to increase your return, dividend strategies can be another.

As an analogy, let's say the two of us make a bet on who can pedal a bicycle at a speed of twenty miles per hour longer. If you took this bet, you'd have two strategies you could implement. First, you could pedal beside me, making this a competition of brute strength. Or you could take the crafty approach and trail *behind* me, benefiting from drafting and conserving 20 to 30 percent of your energy. Then, just as I begin to tire, you can maneuver to the side and overtake me, securing your win.

Going all in with high-risk moves is like trying to out-pedal someone in a sprint. But if you play it smart by utilizing options like dividends and dollar-cost averaging, you choose the crafty approach to help you and your clients win. You're using brainpower over brute force to get ahead with way less work.

I suspect I have partially blown your mind that a high dividend value approach can outperform a growth approach in the stock market over time. Think of that as a single-barreled bazooka in your briefcase. So now I'd like to try to do it again. Ask yourself, *Have I ever met a financial advisor in his or her right mind who would claim that getting 100 percent out of the stock market and into bonds ten years before retirement is the best retirement plan?*

Just like being a math nerd allowed me to prove the value of dividends in common stocks, it will now allow me to back up this statement. Stay with me here; it's going to be a fun ride.

The Double-Barreled Bazooka in Your Briefcase

If you asked your clients whether they preferred a financial plan based on what's likely to happen or merely on hopeful speculation, what response do you think you'd get? Naturally, they'd opt for the plan grounded in reality. Furthermore, if you asked about their retirement savings, questioning whether they intend to spend it all at once, save it for a substantial legacy, or primarily use it to fund their retirement income, the answer is obvious. Essentially, the objective is to optimize the income derived from their retirement funds.

TWO ASSUMPTIONS ABOUT YOUR CLIENTS

Most clients want their money for *income* not for lump sum or inheritance.

Most clients want a plan based on what they *know* is likely true, not what they *hope* is true.

Now consider how most financial advisors have been taught. If a client has a million dollars and plans to retire in ten years, how do we calculate their expected income? We start with a growth assumption, often using 7 percent as a balanced growth rate. If a million dollars grows at 7 percent annually for ten years, they'd end up with $2 million. At this point, they might withdraw using the 4 percent rule or invest in income-generating assets.

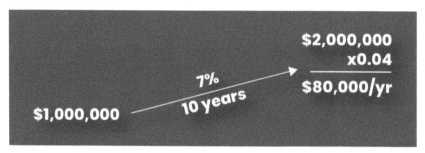

I feel comfortable with the 4 percent figure if we're using income-generating assets. This is because we were able to generate 4 percent interest and dividends, net of fees, in the early 2020s—perhaps the worst interest rate environment in recent history. Therefore, theoretically, $2 million at 4 percent would yield $80,000 annually. But is this projection reliable? If we initiated this plan in 2000, our client would have faced thirteen years of market downturns. Consequently, by 2010, their portfolio might have dwindled to approximately $800,000. Let me ask you: would your clients want to liquidate that $800,000 account to invest in income-producing assets at that stage? For most, the obvious answer is no.

So let's do something completely novel and actually listen to what our client wants. Let's build them a plan on what we *know* is true rather than what we *hope* is true, acknowledging that current dividend yields on the S&P 500 are less than 1.5 percent. A million dollars at this rate generates $15,000 annually. Through reinvestment, this could grow to $18,000 over ten years. If we were completely transparent, we'd admit the potential income range is vast, from $18,000 to $80,000 a decade from now.

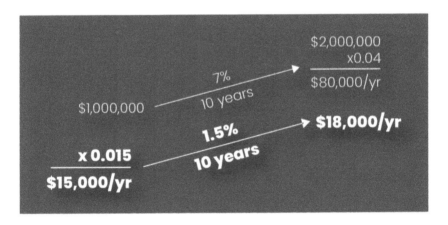

Imagine telling a prospective client, "I've prepared the paperwork to help you with your life savings. But before you sign, I want you to realize that your income ten years from now will be between $18,000 and $80,000 a year using my strategies. So here are the signature pages. Don't forget there are three copies, so press hard."

Do you really think you will earn this client's trust?

A while back, I had an ex–business partner who underwent hemorrhoid surgery, and the doctor informed him he would experience "a little discomfort" as he recovered. However, his doctor didn't share the full details, and three days later, my friend found himself sitting in a bathtub full of ice cubes and in severe pain.

Distraught, he called me, yelling into the phone about the "little discomfort" and expressing his, let's say, *passionate desire* to confront his doctor.

Now here was the challenge. If the doctor had been upfront about the extent of the post-surgery pain, my friend likely would have reconsidered the procedure, and he'd be in worse shape today. Fortunately, he moved forward, and everything worked out in the end (pun intended). However, while downplaying situations is common in every industry, we must not do this with people's life savings.

So once again, we should be committed to listening to our client and developing a plan based on what we *know* to be accurate rather than what we *hope* is true. Suppose we transition clients to income-producing investments, such as bonds, ten years before retirement. Given today's interest rates, a million dollars would generate $50,000 a year in income, net of fees. We also understand that if this $50,000 were reinvested, it would grow 5 percent yearly. Therefore, after ten years, the client's income would have compounded to $80,000, aligning precisely with the high end of the $18,000 to $80,000 range, with minimal variance in outcomes.

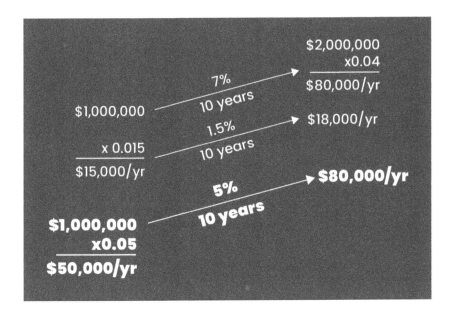

I will candidly inform the client that I am still determining the exact future value of that million dollars in ten years. However, I *can* provide them with a reasonable estimate of their expected income, which again is at the high end of the $18,000 to $80,000 range. But what if interest rates decrease, and we find ourselves in a scenario where the net yield is 4 percent after fees? In that case, the same million dollars would generate $40,000 in net income. Reinvesting that net income for ten years at a 4 percent annual growth rate would result in $60,000 of income. When presented with these scenarios, if you ask your clients whether they would prefer option A (an income range of $18,000 to $80,000 ten years from now) or option B (a fairly precise $60,000 of income), which do you think they would choose?

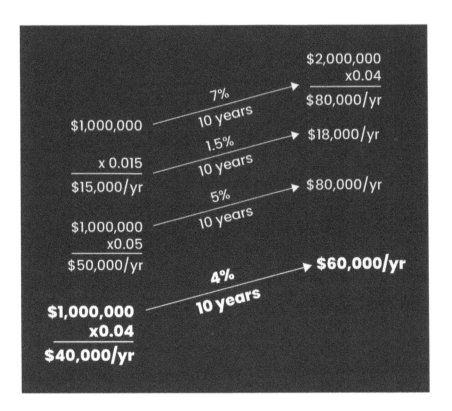

This approach demonstrates how attentively we should listen to our clients. Most have indicated that their primary goal for these funds is retirement and maximizing income, and that's precisely what we should aim to do. They've also expressed a desire to build a plan based on realistic expectations rather than hopeful assumptions, which we've accommodated. So the question arises: *Why is the prevalent teaching in our industry focused on growth, showing a potential increase from $1 million to $2 million, when clients are less concerned with their lump sum balance and more concerned with income?*

The preference for income over a lump sum for purchases and the desire to avoid planning based on hope indicate that clients' needs are often misunderstood. This highlights a simple yet often overlooked concept we've mathematically proven: *transitioning from stocks to bonds ten years before retirement can align more with clients' preferences.* This is not to say we advise everyone to make such a switch; rather, it just shows one more place where the financial services industry falls short when trying to help their clients.

Thankfully, two key strategies can significantly empower financial advisors such as yourself and give you not just a single barrel but a *double-barreled* bazooka in your briefcase.

- Strategy #1: Utilize high-dividend stock strategies for more potential growth with less risk.

- Strategy #2: Demonstrate the mathematical advantage of transitioning to income-generating investments a decade before retirement.

Can you think of any retired or approaching-retirement client who doesn't want more income with less risk and more return? I can't. Using this new approach to educate people makes you sound different from nearly every competitor. Once again, it's why many of the financial advisors I mentor consistently bring in between $50 and $100 million of new assets every year.

This Approach Still Works

A while back, I spoke at one of our national conferences with all our income specialist advisors in attendance. Stepping onstage, I started with an example that sucked the air out of the building.

My first six slides were copies of announcements from major Wall Street firms that said they were getting into the retirement-income-planning world. As I flipped from one slide to the next, I couldn't help but notice the concerned looks of those in attendance.

Many of them started to think, *Oh my goodness, we've lost our point of differentiation.*

That's when I paused and said, "Cheer up folks! There is one word in all these announcements that tells me these major companies don't know what we know. Do you know what that word is? It's *planning.*"

I went on to explain that, at the end of the day, our business was simple. If clients were engineering income through withdrawals, they needed a plan to lower the chances that they would run out. But if they were living off interest and dividends and not touching their principal, they didn't need a plan because they were essentially living off a renewable resource, not a finite resource.

Whenever I hear the phrase "retirement income plan," I understand the person making this statement just doesn't get it. Now suppose you're an advisor who is big into planning and uses Monte Carlo analysis, or the "buckets of money" approach, to financial investing. In that case, I do not doubt you're helping people minimize their risks. But understand the basic premise of your philosophy. You're still having people withdraw from their principal and hoping their stockpile of money outlives their existence. This might work 90 percent of the time, but that shouldn't be a risk you're willing to take.

Instead, if you want to generate attention for your business and stand apart from the pack, embrace a different financial model that prevents clients from tapping into their principal and helps them live off their interest and dividends. This is the best model for you and them.

When you embrace this new approach, you'll no longer compete against everyone else. This is because every other advisor is competing on a total return basis. *What did you earn last year? What did your competitor earn last year?* And that's ugly because I don't care how good you are at investing money; if you compete on a total return basis, at times, you'll have losses and lose clients because you are viewed as a commodity. The only way for any advisor to eliminate that risk is to change the rules!

If you can refocus your clients' thinking on income and let them focus on the income component of their investments, guess what? When you conduct annual reviews with your clients, you're no longer competing against other financial advisors. You've reframed your clients' thinking that it's not about *total return*. It's about the *income* component of total return.

Picture this: you get a call from a client while the market takes a hit, but you've already got them on an income-first strategy. For those already drawing their income, you reassure them that their cash flow hasn't budged despite the market slump and their portfolio taking a dip. And for the clients still in the accumulation phase, who are reinvesting their earnings, there's a silver lining. You tell them the drop in market prices means they're scooping up more for their money, setting the stage for their future income to increase even faster. Imagine the twist with your clients actually getting excited when the market goes down!

Yes, I know this is a departure from the norm. But if you work with retirees and pre-retirees, I'd encourage you to forget the crystal-ball predictions about whether stocks or bonds, growth stocks or high-dividend value stocks will perform better over the next decade. The reality is *no one* can predict the future with certainty. Instead, why not adopt a model that is backed by mathematical proof?

Use this approach, and I guarantee you'll generate attention that prospects won't ignore.

CHAPTER 3

BRANDING TO PIQUE INTEREST

A*I*DA

If there's one chapter you might be tempted to skip, it's this one.

Branding is a word that makes many financial advisors' eyes glaze over. We know it's probably important, but we think it's a step we can circle back to *after* our company has grown. If this is where you are today, I challenge you to pause and allow this chapter to reshape your thinking.

Regardless of the industry, *every* major corporation in America knows that marketing has two components: lead generation and branding. Unfortunately, in the financial services industry, we often forget about that second part. Maybe it's because we're too impatient. We get so focused on the whole "butts in the seat" approach to business we've developed from various marketing approaches such as workshops that we forget to brand. But this is a huge mistake because, intuitively, we know branding is critical.

Branding is about education. If you have an area of specialty, which is the first step of the AIDA formula, branding educates the consumer on why that specialty is so important to them. It's developing a clear and compelling value proposition that distinguishes your brand from competitors by clearly articulating what makes it unique and why your brand is the best choice for your target audience. It isn't just about the quality of products or services but also your brand's unique benefits and experiences.

Think about Big Pharma. This industry spends heavily on branding to differentiate its drugs, build trust, and influence prescriptions. Why do they do this? Because they're trying to educate us to associate their medications with the cures for what ails us. Then, the next time we go to the doctor, we ask for their drugs of choice.

Branding makes the sale easier. If you're well-branded and people know your identity, your lead-generation efforts will be more effective, and your closing ratio will be much higher, as you are perceived as the safer alternative to your competition. While you might be tempted to think prospects don't care about the strength of your brand, this is not the case. As Donald Miller writes in *Building a StoryBrand*, "People want your brand to participate in their transformation."[6] They're looking at the financial services you offer and assessing whether you fit into one of the most crucial parts of their life's journey.

By crafting a compelling brand story and consistently communicating it across all touchpoints, your business can forge emotional connections with consumers, ensuring long-term success and sustainability. In short, when you have a trusted brand, people feel safe and are attracted to you. But when you have a weak brand, prospects start to run.

---

6   Donald Miller, *Building a StoryBrand: Clarify Your Message So Customers Will Listen* (New York: HarperCollins Leadership, 2017), 131.

Choose Your Doctor

For example, let's say you were to visit me at my corporate head-quarters in Florida. You're enjoying the sunshine and eighty-degree weather (yes, I just had to rub that in), but just as you arrive at our office, you notice some chest pains. Not sure what else to do, you rush with one of our team members to a local doc-in-the-box walk-in clinic around the corner.

As you walk up to the front of the building, you notice the paint is peeling, and one of the letters on the "emergency" sign has fallen off. Walking through the double doors and into the reception area, you can't help but notice a funny smell and a stained carpet. After you hear, "The doctor will be with you shortly," you sit down in the lobby, your chest pounding even harder.

Thirty minutes later, the doctor invites you in for an examination. After a few moments of probing and prodding, he looks at you and says, "Listen, this doesn't look good. You're going to need open heart surgery … today."

Consider what your response might be. If you're like most, chances are, you will want a second opinion. You're in a new community, visiting a new doctor, and receiving a terrible new diagnosis. And just because Mr. Doc-in-the-Box says this is what you need, based on every negative experience you've had so far, you will struggle to believe the source.

Now consider an alternative scenario. Let's say you feel those same chest pains, but this time, you drive straight to our local branch of the Cleveland Clinic. The hospital is in pristine condition, and after a series of tests, the doctor comes out and gives you the same prognosis: "You need open heart surgery, and you need it now." Chances are that this time, you will listen and take his advice.

Why? Because you trust the brand.

The Power of Branding

Branding = *Education*

According to Seth Godin, "A brand is the set of expectations, memories, stories and relationships that, taken together, account for a consumer's decision to choose one product or service over another."[7]

The origin of branding can be traced back to ancient times when artisans began to mark their goods to signify the maker's identity and assure quality. This practice evolved from simple maker's marks on pottery in ancient Mesopotamia around 4000 BC to the branding of livestock in Egypt around 2700 BC to differentiate one person's cattle from another's. These early forms of branding were essentially the first attempts to establish a reputation and guarantee the origin of products in the marketplace.

As trade expanded, branding became crucial for distinguishing goods and services and educating consumers. Again, this is why Big Pharma spends so many advertising dollars to build trust with its target audience. Over the centuries, this concept evolved into the complex brand identities and marketing strategies we see today, encompassing not just logos and trademarks but also a company's entire identity and values.

In 2024, branding is more important than ever, and there's a reason why thirty-second Super Bowl commercials cost a whopping total of

---

7   Seth Godin, "Define: Brand," Seth's Blog, December 13, 2009, https://seths. blog/2009/12/define-brand/.

$7 million.[8] Advertisers realize this isn't just about generating more attention for their product. They realize one ad could rebrand their entire company overnight. Branding and lead generation work together.

Branding makes your lead-generation efforts stronger and the sale easier. The better branded you are in your community, the more people will respond to your leads, and the more you will attract serious prospects ready to do business. In the words of Elon Musk, "Brand is just a perception, and perception will match reality over time."[9]

Take, for example, Apple's iconic "1984" Super Bowl ad. Directed by Ridley Scott, this groundbreaking ad aired during Super Bowl XVIII in 1984 to launch the Apple Macintosh computer. The commercial, inspired by George Orwell's dystopian novel *1984*, depicted a heroine running through a dark, oppressive world to smash a screen displaying a Big Brother–like figure, symbolizing Apple's challenge to the conformity and dominance of its competitors, notably IBM.[10]

This ad catapulted Apple into the national spotlight and redefined the company as a revolutionary and innovative force in the technology industry, emphasizing creativity and individuality. The "1984" commercial is often credited with setting a new standard for Super Bowl advertising. It was a pivotal moment in Apple's brand evolution, transforming it from a relatively unknown company to a key player in the tech world.

---

8   Statista, "Total Advertisement Revenue of Super Bowls," https://www.statista.com/statistics/217134/total-advertisement-revenue-of-super-bowls/.

9   Ananya Bhattacharya, "5 Elon Musk Quotes about Innovation," Inc.com, accessed March 25, 2024, https://www.inc.com/ananya-bhattacharya/5-elon-musk-quotes-about-innovation.html.

10   Mac History, "Apple's 1984 Super Bowl Commercial (HD)," video, YouTube, February 1, 2012, https://www.youtube.com/watch?v=VtvjbmoDx-I&ab_channel=MacHistory.

What Does and Doesn't Work

According to Donald Miller, author of *Building a StoryBrand*, there are two major mistakes brands make. "The first mistake brands make is they fail to focus on the aspects of their offer that will help people survive and thrive."[11] He continues, "The second mistake brands make is they cause their customers to burn too many calories in an effort to understand their offer."[12]

In the '90s, I focused on the inverse approach of this second mistake and offered prospects calorie-filled dinner seminars. This posturing worked well at the time because many prospects thought, *Wow, if this guy can feed all of us, he must be the real deal.* This approach gave me instant credibility. Similarly, I also remember sending out tons of mailers. These did double duty because they generated leads and branded my public image as "the income specialist guy."

Fast-forward a couple of decades, and times have changed. As mentioned previously, I discovered dinner seminars were less effective and de-postured more than they postured me. However, I also realized there were some steps I could take that clearly communicated the main message of my brand while not making prospects consume too many calories to understand what I was talking about. Here are three approaches you might find helpful.

APPROACH #1: TRADITIONAL BRANDING

One of our advisors, Greg, from Oklahoma, invested in radio ads. Even though it took him five years before he saw financial returns, this

---

11   Donald Miller, *Building a StoryBrand: Clarify Your Message So Customers Will Listen* (New York: HarperCollins Leadership, 2017), 7.

12   Donald Miller, *Building a StoryBrand: Clarify Your Message So Customers Will Listen* (New York: HarperCollins Leadership, 2017), 8.

became a critical growth factor in his business, and he now generates over $80 million a year in new business from these ads.

Another option is to create your own radio show. Sure, you'll need to invest in airtime, but don't overlook the power of radio shows for drumming up business and building your brand. You could sprinkle in calls to action during your show—offering free books or reports or promoting your workshops. This approach not only elevates your brand but also reels in potential clients who reach out for a freebie or a chat, setting the stage for you to follow up. To give you an idea of the potential here, one of our advisors, Mark, brought in $80 million annually just from his radio show. It's a clear example of how a single platform can significantly bolster both your brand and your client base over time.

As mentioned, offering freebies, such as books you've authored, on your radio show can be very effective. Because many of our advisors are published authors, they have instant credibility with others. This becomes a great way to posture and build their brands. For example, we have an advisor, Jeff, from Florida, who was doing a great job bringing in probably $15 to $20 million a year before he published his first book. But after he wrote one, his business shot up to over $50 million of new assets within a year.

And let's not forget PR. Regular appearances on radio or TV can do wonders for your visibility without breaking the bank. I recently chatted with a man named Ed from Delaware. He's one of our advisors, and as he shared on my podcast, *The Elevated Advisor*, he brought in $150 million in new assets in 2023 through consistent TV appearances. It's proof that with the right strategy and some patience, PR can be an incredibly effective branding and lead-generation tool— assuming you're comfortable in the spotlight.

APPROACH #2: AFFORDABLE BRANDING

Following the COVID-19 pandemic, prospects become much more comfortable with online research. Now, before they attend a workshop or seminar, they do their homework. This is why it's imperative to have an effective online presence. The last thing you want is for a potential client to search for someone with your area of specialty only to go with one of your competitors because your brand doesn't rise to the top of the search page.

This speaks to the importance of SEO, or search engine optimization. You've instantly got an edge if you're the first name a potential client sees when searching for advice. Similarly, leveraging social media—even TikTok—for educational videos can massively boost your brand for little to no cost. Building authentic connections with your audience through "organic branding" on platforms like Facebook, YouTube, and Instagram is crucial because it lets you engage directly without the costs of paid ads.

You cultivate a loyal community by showcasing your brand's personality, values, and offerings in content that truly resonates. Whether through relatable posts and stories on Facebook and Instagram or valuable, informative videos on YouTube, you're enhancing visibility and reputation via shares, likes, and comments. This approach strengthens your bond with your community, fostering a supportive environment where word-of-mouth and viral marketing thrive, ultimately supporting your brand's long-term growth and credibility.

Also, you can use social media platforms "inorganically." You could pay to market and generate leads on most of these platforms. Additionally, as a call to action, you could have the opportunity to click on a Calendly, an online calendar, and schedule an appointment with you. For example, we've seen folks pull off Social Security appointments for under one hundred dollars—a real bargain considering the impact. Imagine, with just a simple click on a Calendly link from an ad, people are lining up appointments with you at a fraction of the usual cost. And while Social Security topics are a hit, the strategy works across the board. It's a dual-threat approach: boosting your brand while funneling leads directly to your doorstep, all with remarkable efficiency.

Podcasts are a cheaper version of radio. They offer a unique and effective form of branding due to their ability to create a personal connection with the audience. Through engaging storytelling and the intimate nature of audio content, brands can convey their values, personality, and knowledge directly to listeners. This format allows for deep dives into topics, showcasing a brand's authority and building trust with an audience over time. Additionally, podcasts can reach audiences during moments when other forms of media can't—such as while driving or exercising—making them a versatile tool in your marketing arsenal.

APPROACH #3: DOUBLE-DUTY BRANDING

One of the best forms of branding is what I call "double-duty branding." This allows you to make the most out of your marketing efforts by simultaneously enhancing your brand awareness and driving lead generation. By embedding your brand's value proposition and identity into every marketing activity, you can attract potential customers while solidifying your position in the market.

Two practical ways to do this include webinars and workshops. You can host webinars on a variety of topics that interest consumers. Additionally, consider organizing non-dinner workshops by renting a room in libraries, schools, or other public facilities. Prospects feel safer attending these workshops because they believe you have some endorsement from the community. You're viewed as a trustworthy and safe choice for them to listen to and engage with. Activities like webinars and workshops perform a double duty because now you're connecting with the same group of people every few months. In the process, you're generating leads while increasing your brand's strength.

> There are a million ways to brand. The key is to brand yourself in a way that *attracts* instead of *chases*.

Then there are adult education courses, an absolute gem for marketing. I started offering these in the late '90s, and it's still effective. When you teach a course, you're not just a name in the catalog; you become an authority. Pair this with targeted mailers, and you've got a recipe for brand visibility and lead generation. Plus, offering a free consultation as part of the course fee can convert education into engagement.

In essence, these methods aren't just about getting your name out there; they're about creating opportunities for direct engagement with potential clients, showcasing your experience, and building trust in your brand.

It's about Posture

There are a million ways to brand. The key is to brand yourself in a way that *attracts* instead of *chases*. While methods always evolve, branding, at its core, is about establishing and nurturing a relationship between a business and its customers. As Jeff Bezos notes, "A brand for a company is like a reputation for a person."[13] Despite changes in marketing and advertising, there are foundational principles of branding that remain timeless. Here are five key principles that never change:

Consistency: In business, unsuccessful people try things to see *if they work*. On the other hand, successful people often do things *until they work*. That's why consistency is crucial in a well-developed branding strategy. This means maintaining a cohesive identity and message

---

13   https://www.brainyquote.com/quotes/jeff_bezos_173309.

across all platforms and touchpoints with your audience. Consistency helps build recognition and trust over time, making your brand more memorable and reliable in the eyes of consumers. While I didn't see instant results, when I consistently educated my people on the benefits of income, this eventually led to a ten-fold increase in my business. This underscores the reality that persistence is key to success; those who achieve it often stick with their strategies until they pay off. Remember Greg? It took him five years of radio advertising, but eventually, it paid off in spades. You have the potential to do the same. If someone else has achieved success through persistence, there's no reason you can't as well.

Emotional Connection: Successful brands go beyond transactions; they connect with their customers on an emotional level. This connection can stem from shared values, desires, or aspirations, making the brand more than just a provider of goods or services but a part of the customer's identity or lifestyle. I've already mentioned podcasts as a great tool. Still, the key is consistently sharing relatable insights and stories and becoming a familiar presence in your prospects' daily lives, fostering a strong emotional bond over time. Again, podcasts, radio shows, or having a book are unique ways to build strong connections. People feel like they know you.

Value Proposition: Again, a clear and compelling value proposition is essential. It distinguishes your brand from competitors by clearly articulating what makes it unique and why it is the best choice for your target audience. This isn't just about the quality of products or services but also your brand's unique benefits and experiences.

Authenticity: This resonates with audiences. Brands that are genuine in their communications, promises, and actions forge stronger, more meaningful relationships with consumers. This includes being transparent, honest, and true to the brand's values and mission. It solidifies that emotional connection and helps prospects get to know you as a real person.

Adaptability: While this may seem counterintuitive to the idea of consistency, adaptability refers to the ability of a brand to evolve with its market, audience, and cultural trends without losing its core identity. This ensures the brand remains relevant and can sustain long-term growth and loyalty.

These principles serve as the foundation for building a strong, enduring brand that can navigate changes in the market, consumer behavior, and technology while maintaining a deep and lasting connection with your audience.

Don't Avoid Branding

Building a great brand or reputation takes time. As Warren Buffett writes, "It takes 20 years to build a reputation and five minutes to ruin it."[14]

I challenge you to not let the immediate allure of lead generation overshadow the enduring benefits of branding. Whether you're authoring a book, engaging in PR activities, optimizing for search engines, teaching adult education classes, hosting radio shows, or any other strategy we've discussed, remember that branding should *always* be at the core of your efforts.

Neglecting branding is like resigning yourself to an endless cycle of pursuit. It's exhausting and leads to burnout. Today, I urge you to identify at least one branding activity you can initiate without breaking the bank. Start building your brand now and always vow to recognize its critical role.

Only through effective branding can you generate proper interest in your prospects.

---

14   James Berman, "The Three Essential Warren Buffett Quotes to Live By," *Forbes*, April 20, 2014, https://www.forbes.com/sites/jamesberman/2014/04/20/the-three-essential-warren-buffett-quotes-to-live-by/?sh=6c137d3b6543.

CHAPTER 4

GENERATING LEADS AND SPARKING DESIRE

A*I*D*A*

These systems aren't new, nor are they rocket science. Maybe you tried these and some worked but some didn't. For those that didn't, it's probably because you didn't know the secret sauce necessary for them to work. The key is persistence. Unfortunately, many people give up before they discover the secret sauce.

After you've developed some *attention* and *interest*, it's time to take your prospects to the next level and spark *desire*. As you do this, you will start to generate leads. This involves engaging potential clients to the point where they are eager to initiate a conversation.

Attraction-based lead generation is more than just about *attracting* leads. It's about *engaging* them in a way that fosters genuine interest and desire to interact with your services. Many firms offer appointment-setting services that "generate leads," leading you to think you're attracting prospects. But the truth is that most of these services are chasing-based approaches. It wasn't as though somebody was interested in the service you had to offer. Instead, it's more likely they just happened to click on something, and now they're receiving a barrage of calls from you and other advisors.

The goal of effective lead generation isn't just to get random strangers' contact information. The goal is to have a *conversation* with a clear prospect who has noticed your brand and believes you have a better service than other options available. Your branding efforts educated them, and now they're interested. But now they have to raise their hands to have a one-on-one conversation.

There are two primary ways to generate leads: time and money. If you have more time on your hands, one way to generate leads is to use some elbow grease and make things happen. Or, if you don't have as much time, you can write a check and spend money instead. Your approach depends on where you are in your career and what's more important to you.

Regardless of your approach, the key is to use lead generation to spark your prospects' desire to have a one-on-one conversation with you. But don't put all your eggs in one basket. The key is to diversify your approaches. Just as a golfer has up to fourteen clubs in her bag, you need multiple attraction-based lead-generating systems.

Bull's-Eye Marketing

This brings us to a model I call "bull's-eye marketing." In the early 2000s, I structured study groups for our advisors to learn and brainstorm with each other. These types of groups historically boosted my development as a producer. With our advisors, I acted as a moderator, allowing me to see the real problems our advisors faced. One session was particularly memorable. By then, we had more than twenty lead-generation systems to offer, in addition to our dinner seminars that some of our more successful advisors were still doing. However, soon after we started, a common complaint emerged as the advisors started grumbling about dinner seminars. They griped about how most prospects who attended were just "plate lickers"—those not interested in the services being offered but hesitant to change to the other system.

I sat silently for a few moments, but soon, I grew frustrated and had enough. I stopped them and said, "Guys, you're all sitting here crying like a bunch of babies. You're all so focused on dinner seminars when we all know they represent a chasing methodology. You know we have dozens of other attraction-based lead-generation systems that are cheaper or give you warmer leads than dinner seminars."

The irony was that, despite knowing we offered these attraction-based lead-generation systems, they had become addicted to dinner seminars because this was what they were used to. As a result, they were banging their heads against a wall—feeling the pain but lacking the resolve to change. This behavior is part of human nature.

Noticing the confused look on these advisors' faces, I continued. "Here's what we're going to do," I told them. "Nobody is leaving my dining room until you pick at least three systems you want to use next year."

From there, I took out our dining room whiteboard (yes, Teresa, my better half, is a saint for allowing me to have one in this room) and drew a giant bull's-eye with six rings. The center represented the warmest or most effective lead generation techniques, and rings two through six represented progressively colder or more expensive approaches. Within a few minutes, I'd written nearly thirty alternatives to dinner seminars on the board and connected them with which rings they represented.

Ironically, dinner seminars fell in the fifth ring as colder and more expensive. I shared with these advisors the advice I've already shared with you in this book. "If you are bribing someone with a steak dinner to listen to you, you are chasing. You know it, and they know it."

While a well-planned, well-executed public dinner seminar can still be a valuable prospecting tool, they have become more difficult in recent years. Increased competition among advisors has made prospects discriminatory and seminars a "tougher sell." With attendance shrinking, it now takes more mailers (meaning more money) to attract the same number of people you were getting with fewer mailers three years ago. The vast majority of qualified prospects will never attend a public dinner seminar. Also, one needs to be a really good presenter to convert an attendee from being a chasee to wanting to chase you.

The problem in my dining room that day was that our advisors had become so addicted to dinner seminars as the primary tool for lead generation that they simply resisted change. This evening became a turning point for Advisors' Academy. It helped our members diversify their lead generation methods and significantly improved asset accumulation. This success led to establishing the "$50 million framework," which represents the amount of new assets that many of our advisors gather annually.

Here is what the breakdown of these six rings looks like.

BULL'S-EYE MARKETING

RING 6: OLD AND COLD

This outer ring represents outdated tactics with diminishing returns. Advisors relying on these cold tactics for lead generation are playing a numbers game in which it is becoming increasingly difficult to break even, let alone win. With potential prospects becoming more discriminatory and the cost of everything from postage to food always rising, the odds of getting a meaningful return on any of these marketing investments are generally slim.

Direct Mail: One example of a sixth-ring approach is direct mail. This is one of the oldest and coldest lead-generation methods, but it is also one of the least cost-effective and most labor-intensive.

Telemarketing and Third-Party Leads: Other examples of old-and-cold methods include vendor or third-party leads and telemarketing strategies. These are generally cold and relatively expensive prospecting approaches in a competitive field where the results can be hit or miss.

Also, as referenced earlier, remember that these efforts from digital marketing agencies that drive strangers to set up a Calendly appointment with you might sound good in theory but often deliver little in lasting value.

RING 5: THE STANDBY

Dinner Seminars: Enough said.

RING 4: ATTRACT OR LEVERAGE

The goal of the fourth ring of lead generation strategies is to draw eager audiences and warm prospects by providing a necessary service. The programs here set you above the competition by putting you in front of targeted groups of warm prospects in ways that earn you instant credibility and respect, often by providing a necessary service without ever buying a meal. Here are a few examples of the fourth ring's approaches.

TaxPro: While attracting prospects by offering a tax service is not new, the proprietary TaxPro system is unique and dramatically more effective than any other tax model available. It's entirely turnkey and requires no previous tax experience.

College Planning: Around 19 million students seek to attend college each year, and it's up to their parents to figure out how to pay for it.[15] You can help them reallocate assets to increase financial aid and demonstrate why life insurance or annuities are perfect strategies

---

15   Melanie Hanson, "College Enrollment Statistics [2024]: Total + by Demo-
      graphic," Education Data Initiative, August 31, 2024, https://educationdata.org/
      college-enrollment-statistics.

because they don't undercut financial assistance eligibility. This necessary and appreciated service puts you in an excellent prospecting position.

Federal Employee Benefits Specialist: Here, you can help government employees in a particular community understand their benefits. Again, this is a necessary service that puts you in a great position to identify qualified prospects.

Adult Education: Teaching a financial course through a local community college or high school's adult education program is like hosting a public seminar without all the expense. As the teacher, you are automatically better postured than any seminar host—and you know your audience is there to learn, not eat!

Non-Dinner Workshops in a Public Venue: These public venues could include the library, a community center, or a school. There, you can offer options such as estate planning workshops, Social Security educational workshops, or required minimum distribution (RMD) educational workshops.

Estate planning workshops are a popular way to help retirees and near-retirees understand why estate planning encompasses not just wills and trusts but also the accumulation and preservation of their assets.

Social Security educational workshops are popular among baby boomers who are eager for expert guidance to help them learn how to maximize their Social Security benefits, focusing on the importance of having the right asset allocation for taking Social Security.

RMD educational workshops help retirees who know little about their required minimum distributions and are eager to learn. You can provide this much-needed service and posture yourself as a financial educator qualified to help them understand whether their asset allocation is right for taking RMDs.

Webinar Workshops: While you can cover the same topics you'd cover in non-dinner workshops, webinars help you cast a wider net geographically, making your content accessible to anyone in the world.

Lead Generation Websites: A state-of-the-art website positions you as a financial visionary who can provide an important public service by educating clients and the public about protecting their assets in today's challenging economic climate.

RING 3: CENTERS OF INFLUENCE

Strategic partnerships with influential figures put you in a perfect position to attract new business. These strategies bring you closer to the bull's-eye by raising your brand awareness and credibility through partnerships with trusted, influential figures and organizations—both nationally and in the communities where your clients (and potential new clients) live and work.

Professional Partnerships: This strategy makes you "the go-to guy" for a local attorney, CPA, or property and casualty specialist whenever one of his clients needs a financial advisor's services. As you may know, many referral relationships don't work because they are not mutually beneficial; often, the advisor will refer one or two clients, but the partner will not reciprocate. Frequently, the advisor will refer five to ten clients, but the partner will not reciprocate. This is usually because the advisor is coming from a point of weakness in the relationship. Our approach is different because it puts you in a position of strength as a business consultant offering tangible strategies to help your partner grow his business.

Financial Literacy Trainer: Top executives typically get $10,000 to $20,000 a year for financial planning, while the average employee gets nothing. That's why people mismanage their 401(k)s. They don't know the basics of financial planning and are, essentially, financially illiterate. Businesses across America want to provide their employees with some form of expert financial literacy training, but most lack the in-house resources to do so. The odds are that at least one of your clients has worked for such a business and can help you arrange to give a series of financial literacy presentations.

Guest Speaker: Over one million organizations throughout America are seeking speakers for member events. It's likely that one or more of your clients belongs to such an organization and could serve as your liaison for hosting a presentation on a timely financial topic.

PR: When you get interviewed for TV, radio, or print, these mediums make *you* the center of influence. You are presented as a clear authority to the audience and gain instant credibility. A great example is Ed from Delaware, who I mentioned earlier. Through consistent TV appearances, he brought in $150 million in new assets in 2023.

Radio in Your Territory: Radio has proven return numbers and can be part of your success story. This is another medium that makes you the center of influence. Because retirees and near-retirees trust talk radio to get their important information, having a presence on your local radio station builds your center of influence.

RING 2: REFERRALS

Referrals are a surefire way to enlist your existing clients in helping you attract new ones. Enlist your existing clients to assist you, directly or indirectly, in arranging meetings with prospects who you know will likely be well worth your time. Properly planned and executed, any one of these methods could, conceivably, net you as many new clients as a large public event but at a fraction of the cost.

Mother Teresa Approach: Unfortunately, many advisors drop the ball when it comes to directly asking for referrals. They have this limiting belief that makes them afraid to ask. They think, *If I'm such* *a big-shot financial advisor, why am I groveling for business?* This used to be my problem. That's why I created my Mother Teresa approach to help clients see that I do what I do because I love it and want to save the world. Taking on this approach gave me the comfort of going ahead and asking for referrals.

Board of Directors: Assemble a board of your best, most loyal clients to meet quarterly to discuss their ideas on how you can improve client service. In this informal setting, you can emphasize how important referrals are to your business and solicit their ideas on how to get more referrals. As "board members," clients feel they now have a vested interest in helping your business grow and invariably start sending you referrals soon after the meeting.

Lunch and Links: This program enables you to host an informal mini seminar with a client and three potential referrals. It provides a good opportunity for a loyal client to advocate on your behalf as they play a complimentary eighteen holes with their three friends.

Client Appreciation Party: Since your clients know you are passionate about protecting their money, they'll know you're sincere about wanting to help their friends and loved ones protect their assets. This program leverages that trust to solicit qualified referrals and offers further incentives as an attractive prize. These events typically generate fifty to two hundred referrals per one hundred attendees.

Select Club: Even within a group, most people like to feel that they are special or part of something "exclusive" or "select." This program taps into that common trait by rewarding a "select" group of your clients (those who have sent you a referral with whom you have met in the past six months) with a fun event and the chance to win a grand prize.

Birthday Party: This more intimate appreciation event focuses on a client's important milestone. It also includes a strategic referral component and a proprietary method for converting attendees into qualified prospects eager to schedule a meeting with you.

Retirement Party: This is similar to the birthday party, but the strategy here involves identifying a client about to retire, organizing the event, and encouraging them to invite friends and colleagues from work. Generally, these are people the client's age who are also near retirement and, therefore, have immediate or impending financial planning needs—in other words, warm prospects.

Mani/Pedi: This is similar to lunch and links but aimed at female clients and built around a complimentary afternoon at the spa with a small group of the client's friends/referrals.

RING 1: EXISTING CLIENTS

Strong client relationships are the cornerstone of the warmest and most effective strategies in bull's-eye marketing. By being visible, accessible, and proactive with your clients, you earn a level of trust and appreciation that can be strategically leveraged to grow your business from the inside out. All of us like to think we are investing 100 percent of most of our clients' money. But in most cases, this is not true. Unfortunately, many salespeople are so interested in meeting with the next potential prospect that they often neglect servicing their existing clients. They ignore the gold that's sitting in their current client base.

Client Survey: A custom-crafted client survey lets your clients know that their input is important while generating a wealth of invaluable information that helps ensure the success of many bull's-eye marketing strategies.

Client Service Program: Creating a client base that wants to sing your praises and send you referrals is a matter of demonstrating your commitment to proactive client service on an ongoing basis. That requires strategy. At our companies, our comprehensive client service program gives you that strategy in a turnkey format. It includes six client service scripts, processes for categorizing clients and scheduling outbound calls, and a proprietary eight-step client review process that guarantees you will never again "walk over" an opportunity for new business or referrals.

Client Reviews: One potential drawback of a strong client relationship is that its "personal" aspect can sometimes get in the way of conducting a thorough, productive client review. Our exclusive eight-step client review process keeps you focused and on task with every client and ensures that you recognize and seize every possible opportunity for new business and referrals. This is the proprietary cornerstone process in bull's-eye marketing that, when properly implemented, keeps your business growing month after month, year after year.

Client Outreach: It's important to stay "in front" of your clients even when you're not physically in meetings, workshops, or appreciation events. We help you do this by maximizing your website, email, "snail mail," social media, and other platforms to share helpful information and updates regularly. Our turnkey strategy also includes monthly newsletters, quarterly greeting cards, and those all-important scripted client service calls. The resounding message you send with a consistent, content-rich client outreach program is the same message illustrated by the bull's-eye marketing target: *Your clients are the center of everything you do!* The inevitable result is threefold: retention, referrals, and sustained business growth from the inside out!

In short, bull's-eye marketing represents strategies to maximize the value of your most important growth resource: your existing clients. It offers the most diverse and innovative array of lead-generation tools in the financial services industry. Each system is strategically designed to maximize your marketing ROI and help you achieve sustained business growth.

Which Three Will You Choose?

Now let's say I were to have you over to my house for a personal white-board session. Where would you say you are? Maybe you're where many of my advisors were fifteen years ago when they were focused on one method that wasn't very effective. You keep trying to make it work but are constantly banging your head against a wall. Believe me, I can be as stubborn as it gets, and I know this feeling all too well.

But as a financial advisor, it's crucial to engage in activities that are effective. I've implemented almost every one of these strategies successfully, and if I can succeed, so can you. I challenge you to sift through the strategies I've outlined and identify which might work for you.

It's possible you've tried many of these approaches and failed. As a result, you think the system doesn't work when you might be missing just one or two key ingredients. I've found that many of these lead generation programs have a secret sauce that can make or break them. Generating leads and increasing desire is more like baking than cooking. When cooking a meal, chances are you won't ruin supper by not having the precise amount of one spice or herb. Baking is a different story. When you make a cake, you must be precise, and substitutes rarely work. So before you give up on one of these methods and assume it doesn't work, ask yourself if there might be something you can tweak to have success.

Again, when it comes to choosing which three methods to use, it comes back to time and money. Develop a clear understanding of where you are at and what you can physically do or afford and make a game plan. Remember, the end goal of generating leads is to spark desire and have that conversation with an interested prospect.

Remain focused on this, and you'll turn those prospects into clients.

CHAPTER 5

CLOSING THE DEAL

*AID*A

If you've been an advisor for over two minutes, I'm guessing you've had this problem.

You meet with a prospect, and it's obvious you're the perfect fit to solve their problems. Over the course of an hour, you put together a list of recommendations that seem perfect. Everything is going smoothly, and, in your mind, the deal is already done. But that's when you hear that dreaded phrase, "Hey, this is all great, but I'd like a few days to think about it." With that, your prospect walks out the door, taking with them your list of brilliant recommendations and just a little piece of your heart.

A week goes by, and you give them a call. The husband answers and apologizes, saying he and his wife haven't had time to discuss it yet. He asks for another week. You agree, but the next time you call, it goes straight to voicemail. A week later, the same thing happens. Now you're in full-on chase mode, and that sinking feeling sets into your stomach. All the careful positioning and effort you put into attracting them is now spoiled as you find yourself in chase mode, desperately trying to regain what you've lost.

You beat yourself up and start to question everything. *Was there something I missed? Did I not communicate the value clearly enough?* The anxiety gnaws at you as you recall the meeting—the way their eyes lit up when you presented your solution, the nods of agreement, the questions that showed they were really considering your recommendations.

In the meantime, your mind is racing with strategies to get back in the game. You contemplate sending a follow-up email that's a bit more assertive but still polite. You consider sweetening the deal, maybe offering a limited-time discount or an additional perk to nudge them back to the table. But you know deep down that the more you chase, the more control you lose. Do you know that feeling?

Yup, I've been there too. Why does that happen? Because you've given them the product or allocation recommendation, so now they have all the control and you've lost the control. How do you fix that? By learning how to get prospects to ACAT transfer money to you without discussing specific products or allocation!

We're Not as Good as We Think

One reason this is a common story for many advisors is that our industry has leaned on outdated sales tactics that are no longer effective.

For example, in my first job at a big insurance company, I was taught to visit clients in their homes. This approach immediately diminished my authority. Then I was instructed to build rapport with insincere salesman talk, which people saw right through. Think about it—your doctor doesn't waste time on small talk. They get straight to the point, asking where it hurts and diagnosing the issue.

Next, I was told to launch into a spiel about my company, vomiting information before the client knew what was in it for them. This was followed by giving proposals for free, a practice which might as well come with a neon sign saying "salesperson." I'd even allow prospects to have multiple meetings with me, wasting my time and indicating my knowledge wasn't valuable. Thankfully, I had a wake-up call and realized my approach was behind the times.

If this is your story, I get it. One reason advisors fall prey to cheap sales tactics is that they think they're better than they are. They believe they're great salespeople, but the reality is that it's often their ego talking. Advisors think, *Just get me in front of someone, and I'll close the deal.*

However, here's something I've noticed. When new advisors join Sound Income Group, and we connect them with qualified prospects, I've noticed that, in the early days, they frequently struggle to close deals. Why? Because before they were operating on a smaller scale and doing limited marketing. They were used to working with hot referrals, the low-hanging fruit, who were eager to sign and weren't used to sitting down with prospects who were skeptical. As a result, they had an overinflated closing ratio. Only when they started actively marketing and generating leads did they realize the process was tougher than they thought.

I say this because this might be where you're at. When you turned to this chapter and saw the title "Closing the Deal," you might have thought to yourself, *Uh, Dave, I already do that quite well, thank you very much.* And maybe you do. Or maybe you're a little too confident in your abilities.

Successful Advisors Have a Defined Process

Answer this question honestly: If I were to call you at 2:00 a.m. tomorrow morning and ask, "How many steps are in your sales process, and what are they?" how would you answer?

Could you immediately rattle off all the steps, or is your process messy? When I ask this question to ten advisors, only one or two usually offer a decent answer. The rest haven't got a clue. They're thinking, *Well, each person is different, and so I tailor my approach each time.* On the surface, this makes sense. What I'm referring to is, instead of having no structure, having flexibility within your structure.

However, the larger your business grows, the more important the process becomes. This is what separates the good from the great. Ask any advisor bringing in $50 million a year or more in new assets, and I guarantee they have a clear process in place. If I called them at 2:00 a.m., they could give me all the key steps that shape how they turn prospects into clients.

Consider Tom Brady. Love or hate him, he was arguably one of the best quarterbacks ever. Was he flexible, and did he adapt to each play? Of course. But he also had a playbook that outlined his first receiver going deep down the middle, his second receiver as an outlet to the left, and his last receiver doing a shuttle pass to the running back. He had flexibility within his structure.

The problem with many advisors is they are *too* flexible. They fly by the seat of their pants with no structure and become ineffective in the process. Others are *all* structure with zero flexibility, which isn't good either. The best approach combines both.

> The larger your business grows, the more important the process becomes.

I'll go back to my golf analogy. If you're faced with a shot one hundred and fifty yards from the hole, you can approach this in many ways. You might use a full seven iron, a hard eight, a soft six, or even a punch out with a two iron to get below a tree branch. But the best golfers still have a process. When they assess their shot, consider the conditions, pick the right club for the right situation, and swing, they do so strategically.

That's how a good sales process should work—structured but adaptable to the situation.

Seven-Step Process

The sales process is where many advisors mess up the attraction process and cause their prospects to run. At Sound Income Group, we use a seven-step sales process that has been extremely effective. This has helped advisors close 70 to 80 percent of new prospects with assets.

STEP #1: FACT-FINDING AND INFORMATION GATHERING

First, gather all relevant information about the prospect's financial situation. This includes their income, expenses, assets, liabilities, and financial goals. Understanding their *current* financial position and *future* aspirations is crucial. Additionally, assess their risk tolerance, investment preferences, and any specific financial challenges they might be facing.

STEP #2: CATEGORIZING THE PROSPECT

Next, treat each prospect differently and understand which category they fall into. How you handle a prospect should differ based on whether they have all their money with one advisor, spread across multiple advisors, or are do-it-yourselfers. You need to quickly assess whether this is a single-advisor prospect, a multiple-advisor prospect, or a do-it-yourselfer and treat each individual accordingly.

The key difference here is how much money you can realistically help them manage. Experienced advisors might see several opportunities right away, but be careful not to overwhelm the prospect by going for too much too soon. If they're a do-it-yourselfer, they're unlikely to hand over full control immediately. The same goes for multiple-advisor prospects—they diversify by advisor to mitigate risk. Only if the prospect has all their assets with a single advisor should you go after all of it from the start. This strategic approach prevents spooking the prospect and keeps the door open for future opportunities.

STEP #3: TRACKS

This step involves making prospects realize they have problematic investments and strategies. Our system has eleven tracks to choose from, depending on their specific situation—like choosing the right golf club for a particular shot.

STEP #4: WEDGES

The wedge phase helps the prospect answer why their current advisor isn't suited to fix their problem or why they can't fix it if they're a do-it-yourselfer. We have sixteen wedges tailored to different advisor models—whether they're independent, annuity-only, or working for a big wirehouse. Wedges refrain from attacking the advisor by explaining that the advisor's business model limits them from solving this problem. The goal is for the prospect to acknowledge that their advisor, or they, can't solve the identified problem.

STEP #5: THE COMMERCIAL

Here, you talk about how great you are and why they should work with you. Many of you might have been taught to do this at the start, but that's a mistake. The prospect doesn't care about your credentials until they understand how you can benefit them. So only present your commercial *after* you've highlighted their significant problem. In our process, the prospect will let you know when they are ready to hear your commercial by asking you for it. In fact, we resist the urge to vomit our commercial onto some unsuspecting prospect. In our process, the prospect must ask us for our commercial before we give it.

STEP #6: THE CLOSE

If you've done a good job with the first five steps, the pivot to step six should involve a simple open-ended question such as, "Where do we go from here? You tell me your next step in solving this problem." This step involves initiating the Automated Customer Account Transfer Service (ACAT) process to transfer the client's accounts to your management formally. The ACAT process is straightforward and doesn't require any specific product or allocation recommendations. Our approach ensures that you maintain a professional boundary while streamlining the transfer process. Think about it—if you are recommending a specific product allocation before you are hired as an advisor, you are posturing yourself as a salesperson.

By focusing solely on the logistics of the transfer, you avoid the complexities and potential conflicts that can arise from making product-specific suggestions. This not only saves time but also keeps the process clean and compliant, allowing clients to transition their accounts smoothly and efficiently without the pressure of immediate investment decisions.

By completing the ACAT transfer, you become the advisor of record or broker of record, officially taking over the management of their financial accounts. This written commitment signifies that the client has hired you and trusts you to handle their investments and financial planning. It's a crucial step that solidifies your professional relationship and allows you to begin implementing tailored financial strategies for their portfolio.

STEP #7: CREATING THE ALLOCATION

Finally, you transition from your role as a salesperson to that of a dedicated financial advisor. In this capacity, your focus shifts to educating your new client about the possible solutions to their problem. You might discuss the risks, potential returns, and the pros and cons of various strategies. You work closely with your new client to develop a tailored asset allocation strategy that aligns with their financial goals, risk tolerance, and time horizon. In our world, it involves educating the new client about the universe of income-generating alternatives.

Sometimes, I've worked through step seven in minutes and sometimes a few meetings. Either way is fine for me, since they have already become a client by transferring assets. Offering too many complementary meetings with prospects hurts your posturing. Still, once somebody becomes a client, it's your duty to invest as much time as it takes for you and the client to concur on recommendations.

7-STEP SALES PROCESS

Step 1
Fact-Finding and Information Gathering

Step 2
Categorizing the Prospect

Step 3
Tracks

Step 4
Wedges

Step 5
The Commercial

Step 6
The Close

Step 7
Creating the Allocation

Learn to Avoid the #1 Problem in Sales

There is one mistake financial advisors make that always ruins their sales. What is this mistake? *They provide the product or allocation solution too early!* They do this before the prospect understands the magnitude of the problem their solution intends to solve.

Human psychology is such that people generally resist change. In financial sales, prospects are more likely to make a change because they have a pain point, not because they're offered a better alternative. They're motivated more by the stick than the carrot. Thus, prospects come to you thinking they might have a *small* problem but that any change you recommend is bigger and scarier. As humans, our caveman brains are designed to focus on the bigger, scarier things to protect us.

If you provide the product or allocation solution too early, the prospect's brain will turn from the problem and focus on your recommendation. This is when they ask for details about fees, commissions, and time commitments. Their brain starts to look for reasons not to make a change. When you understand this natural resistance, you recognize your job is to help prospects realize the extent of their problem and that you can help them solve it.

If you've ever read Neil Rackham's book *SPIN Selling*, it delves into this concept. SPIN is an acronym for four types of questions: situation questions, problem questions, implication questions, and need-payoff questions. I find those middle two especially significant. Problem questions identify a problem, like, "Oh gee, if the market drops, you could lose half your money." Implication questions explore the implications of the problem. For example, if that 50 percent loss happens, you might have to return to work or significantly reduce your spending. What's the personal impact?

> In the first meeting with a prospect, your job is to help them understand that the problem is much bigger than the solution.

In the first meeting with a prospect, your job is to help them understand that the problem is much bigger than the solution. They need to have a personal aha moment and discover that their problem is more significant than they initially thought. This shift in focus makes them see the magnitude of their issue rather than the details of your solution, positioning **YOU**, not your products as the essential answer to their needs.

Consider this analogy: If you're preparing for elective surgery, you'll want to know every detail—how long recovery will take, how much pain you will be in, how much scarring, and so on. However, if you were in a car accident and lying on the ground bleeding to death, you wouldn't be asking the doctor if he's going to use stitches, staples, or surgical glue. The problem is enormous at that moment, and all you care about is being saved. The same principle applies to sales. When prospects truly grasp the severity of their problem, they focus less on the specifics of their solution and more on the necessity of addressing the issue immediately.

This isn't about using scare tactics or creating problems where none exist; it's about helping prospects identify the true implications of the issues they already have. Often, people only realize the severity of their financial problems once it's properly framed for them.

Building trust through understanding is crucial. Clients who feel that you genuinely understand their problems are more likely to trust you with their assets. By following this approach, you can guide clients through a sales process that emphasizes their needs and concerns, leading to stronger relationships and more successful outcomes.

Swing Thoughts When Meeting with a Prospect

In golf, how you swing determines the effectiveness of your game. While there is a large physical component, the mental side of the game is just as important. When approaching a ball, your mindset is often the determining factor between a straight shot down the fairway and shanking a shot off to the side.

Swing thoughts in golf are mental cues or simple reminders you use to focus on specific aspects of your swing during play. The same is true for advisors, and here are six swing thoughts I'd recommend that will clarify your focus as you prepare to close a deal.

SWING THOUGHT #1: MAKE ONE DECISION AT A TIME

To close a deal, every prospect you encounter must make four crucial decisions. They need to decide that they have bad investments that need changing, and they need to fire their current advisor, hire you, and buy the great whizzbang portfolio you recommend. Simple, right? Not quite, because the human brain can only make one decision at a time. Multiple decisions can be overwhelming if tackled all at once. However, we can separate them. The first and fourth are investment-related, while the second and third are about choosing advisors.

A key aspect of closing any deal is to simplify the process. If you are closing for the ACAT transfer, the client only needs to make two decisions: a) fire their current advisor and b) hire you. When you simplify the process for prospects, you significantly reduce the chance of them hitting you with the "I want to think about it" objection because they're not overwhelmed by making multiple decisions at once. The decisions regarding which assets to sell in their current portfolio and which strategies to implement can be made *after* they become your client.

SWING THOUGHT #2: DISCOVERY PROCESS

As motivational speaker and author Brian Tracy often says, "Telling is not selling."[16] While you might think telling someone they need to lower their risk, get more income, or make a change would be enough to convince them, I can assure you it's not. When you tell someone something, they have two options: agree or disagree.

---

16   https://quotefancy.com/quote/778319/
      Brian-Tracy-Telling-is-not-selling-Only-asking-questions-is-selling.

If they disagree, you end up butting heads. After a couple of objections, it starts to feel contentious. That's not attraction; that's chasing and doing battle. So telling is not selling. Instead, you must lead people through a discovery process where they realize they have a problem and discover that you are the solution.

SWING THOUGHT #3: AVOID PRODUCT BREATH AT ALL COSTS

This is essential if you want people to focus on the *P* and not the *S*. If you start to talk about products or recommended allocations before the ACAT transfer, you will be transferring their attention to the *S*. Think about how many times people might say, "We are with you. You make so much sense. What do you recommend?" ... And you take the bait, but then you hear the all-so-famous objection, "I want to think about it."

If you lead with the product or recommendation, they might go home and google it, and who knows what might pop up. It could be enough to place doubt in their minds and lose confidence in your abilities. Now you've forfeited control, and they've gained it. So avoid discussing specific products before prospects become clients.

SWING THOUGHT #4: PROCESS, NOT PRODUCT

How do you do this? By focusing on the *process* instead of the *product*.

Inevitably, a prospect is going to ask you what you would recommend for them, and your natural inclination is to give a product or allocation answer. Instead, respond with a process answer. As advisors, we naturally think in terms of products because that's how we get paid; it's crucial to shift this mindset. Instead, the next time a prospect asks for your recommendations, try responding to them with something like this:

Do you mean what I would recommend if you were a client of mine? If so, I'd recommend the following process. The first step is for me to become your advisor of record because I can't help you until I am. Then we will roll up our sleeves and get to work. My philosophy is simple: *carve out the cancerous parts and keep the good ones.* This helps ensure that if something goes wrong in the financial markets, at least you are somewhat protected. Then I will invest time in you as a new client, educating you about possible solutions. We will discuss the pros and cons, risks, and returns of each option and build the portfolio together. Only when we both agree that the allocation is right will we implement it.

Always remain focused on the process.

SWING THOUGHT #5: JUDO, NOT KARATE

Financial sales should be more like judo and less like karate.

Most people approach sales with a karate mindset. In my first year in the business, I was taught, "Dave, if you want to get better at closing, you need to get better at overcoming objections." But that's bad advice. Overcoming objections is like doing karate—blocking and punching, blocking and kicking. An objection is a symptom of a problem that arose earlier in the sales process. *Do you want to treat the symptom or the problem?* I prefer treating the problem and addressing something that went wrong earlier in the process because financial sales shouldn't be about force. Instead, it should be like judo, where you entice someone to lean toward you and then use their momentum to your advantage.

How do you do that? By asking strategic questions. We've all been taught that open-ended questions are better than closed-ended questions in sales. But if I had to choose one type of question for sales, I'd pick closed-ended questions. Why? Because with open-ended questions, you don't know if the answer will get them leaning toward you. But by asking enough closed-ended questions, like "Do you prefer A or B?" or "Would you choose C or D?" you're more likely to get at least one answer that creates momentum toward you. This is where you can begin to use judo.

Using this approach, you avoid confrontation and guide the client through a smooth, collaborative process. This builds rapport and trust, making the sales process more effective and less adversarial.

SWING THOUGHT #6: POSTURING

Imagine you walk into a meeting, and the prospect is figuratively, if not literally, sitting with arms folded, thinking, *I wonder what this woman has for me today.*

In their mind, they hold the power because they're the ones with the money, and you're just the salesperson seeking their business. You have one meeting to change that dynamic so they're not looking down at you but looking up to you and thinking, *Wow, I need this advisor's help more than she needs me.* You achieve this by focusing immediately on their problem. Your posture improves once they realize they have a significant issue and that you genuinely care about solving it.

However, many advisors ruin their posturing in various ways, and this is when the attraction process ends, and they resort to chasing. Unknowingly, they do something that puts a red flashing light over their head that says they're a salesperson instead of an advisor. They start meetings with too much small talk. But circling back to my earlier point, financial professionals, like doctors and lawyers, don't waste time with small talk; they get straight to the point. Salespeople often provide free proposals and house calls, while professionals do not. A lawyer might give one free consultation, but after that, you're paying. Salespeople will give multiple free meetings, diluting their perceived value. These actions signal that you're a salesperson, not a trusted advisor. To posture yourself correctly, you need to do the opposite.

Develop the Right Mindset

Several years ago, I owned a custom fishing lure company. Both my number-one competitor and I sold lures for fifteen dollars. My competitor manufactured their product in China for five dollars, while I made mine in the US for ten dollars.

Place yourself in my shoes and ask yourself what a smart businessperson should do first. Should I spend a bunch of money on marketing to sell more lures at a five-dollar profit or first try to maximize profit margins by reducing manufacturing costs to make a ten-dollar profit? The answer is obvious: any businessperson would want to maximize their profit margins first.

In financial sales, your profit margins are your conversion ratios. Every lead-generation initiative will become more

> To effectively close deals is the best thing you can do to scale your business.

profitable by getting better at closing. Thus, learning to effectively close deals is the best thing you can do to scale your business.

Ultimately, you've got to believe in what you're selling. For our advisors, this means truly understanding why income is beneficial. It's embracing that Mother Teresa mindset I referenced earlier that says the only people who matter at this moment are the prospects in front of them. When you're sitting across from a prospect, your job is to convince them to fix their problem, whether they do it with you or someone else. If you can adopt this mindset, even if it feels a bit like "fake it till you make it," you'll be in a strong position. It's about being fully present and genuinely committed to helping them, which clients can sense and appreciate.

It's believing that "Closing this deal is in the best interest of my prospect." The goal isn't just to close the deal and make a sale. It's to make someone else's life better. If an advisor doesn't believe this, their prospects will certainly not believe it. This is why, when you go into a one-hour meeting, you must suppress any desperation—whether it's the pressure of needing a sale to pay your mortgage or any other stress—and do what Tony Robbins suggests and get yourself in the right frame of mind.

> At the end of the day, marketing is an art, not a science.

Like the sailfish, which instinctively swims away when he senses something isn't right, prospects can sense desperation. And the more you can distance yourself from desperation, the more people will realize they need you more than you need them. Again, with our egos, we often think we're great at closing deals. But I can't stress enough that this step is where advisors can ruin the attraction process and slip into chasing mode. At the end of the day, marketing is an art, not a science. You can do everything right, but if circumstances are unfavorable, you may not get many leads. For example, I had a seminar scheduled for September 11, 2001, but the tragedy of that day meant I had to adapt.

However, I've always believed that if I could get in front of one person a week and convert them into a client, I could be successful. This belief brings a certain amount of swagger and an entirely different approach to meetings. In time, I stopped entering meetings trying to convince prospects to sign with me and instead started evaluating if I *wanted* to take them on as my clients.

This is the place you want to be.

PART II:

Practical Application

CHAPTER 6

DEVELOPING YOUR $50 MILLION TEAM

Is it possible to make $1,000 an hour?

This was a question I asked myself five years into my career. After hitting one wall after the next, I decided to spend a few days off by myself and set some goals. While everyone's spot of inspiration differs, my place of choice was Nantucket Island. It was the middle of summer, and for seventy-two hours, I spent most of my afternoons sitting at the end of a beach and working on my goals.

As I did, I remembered that statistic I'd heard in the early nineties that an advisor's time is worth $500 to $1,000 an hour when they're face-to-face, knee-to-knee, elbow-to-elbow with a qualified prospect. I multiplied each of those numbers by forty hours a week and fifty weeks a year and realized this equated to $1 and $2 million a year. And I asked myself, *Why am I earning just a fraction of that?* The answer was that I wasn't spending nearly forty hours a week in front of prospects. Instead, I was bogged down with many duties that weren't giving me the value of the time I desired.

This self-doubt stemmed from my many limiting beliefs, making me feel this was entirely out of reach. There were too many things only I knew how to do. Or so I thought. In my mind, I was the best at tasks like calling referrals and client services. Sure, maybe I could offload some of my paperwork responsibilities, but even that was a struggle.

But sitting on that beach and soaking in the warm summer air, I knew something needed to change. More specifically, I knew *I* needed to change. If I wanted to become an advisor worth $1,000 an hour and make $2 million a year, I had to refocus my efforts and spend all my time on $1,000 an hour of work. To do this, I realized I needed to create a team of four people.

While it took several years to assemble this team, I finally hit that mark and could focus all my efforts on the activities that mattered most. Today, I call this core group of people a "$50 million team."

$50 Million Team

Building a practice that generates $50 million a year in new assets is impossible on your own. You've got to have a team, and this team ideally consists of four different people. Each member performs a distinct role, and each is critical to helping you spend your days doing the work that matters most. You need a mix of team members who are detail-oriented and those who possess strong people skills.

Now chances are that if you're flying solo today, you can't afford to hire all four individuals in one shot, but you *can* start with one and branch out from there. We'll address how to phase your business into the four-person team, but let's start by identifying those four positions.

POSITION #1: NEW BUSINESS PROCESSOR

The first hire often handles new business, manages transfers, and processes all necessary paperwork. For instance, when dealing with an ACAT transfer, they process the transfer paperwork and then actively chase down the transfer. Sometimes, this involves calling the originating firm to expedite the movement of funds.

When allocating investments outside of a brokerage account, such as an annuity or a private placement investment, additional steps are required. The ACAT typically moves funds into a brokerage account. If the allocation is outside this securities account, a second transfer must be processed into the private placement or annuity from the brokerage account.

Assuming you've hired someone proficient in handling all this paperwork, this process will save you countless hours. Ideally, this person will sit with new clients to complete the paperwork, submit it, and follow up to ensure the funds are transferred. Then they may need to repeat this process after the allocation meeting, which is step seven of the sales process.

Essentially, the new businessperson's role, which I often call the "money chaser," involves managing all logistical and paperwork tasks associated with these transactions.

POSITION #2: APPOINTMENT SETTER

Next, we have what we call an appointment setter or marketing person. This role is essential for keeping your calendar filled with prospects and coordinating any marketing efforts. If you use our referral strategies, the appointment setter must organize the referral events. When you partner with centers of influence, like CPAs and attorneys, the appointment setter arranges and confirms those meetings.

If you are hosting a workshop, the appointment setter is responsible for setting up the workshop, managing the marketing, and handling all related logistics. They also follow up on the phone to ensure your calendar remains full. Additionally, the appointment setter monitors the effectiveness of marketing campaigns and adjusts strategies as needed to maximize engagement and attendance. They maintain a detailed database of potential clients and referral sources, ensuring that no opportunity for a connection is missed.

An appointment setter's role is critical in ensuring your calendar is filled with qualified prospects, so you have $1,000-an-hour work all week long.

POSITION #3: CLIENT SERVICE ADVISOR

The third role is that of a client service person. In smaller practices, this might initially be an unlicensed individual handling paperwork and administrative tasks. However, a licensed client service person is ideal because they can discuss accounts and investments with clients, not just handle changes of beneficiary forms or transaction requests. A licensed person can conduct reviews with clients and provide comprehensive service.

You might need two client service people if your clientele is large enough. In this case, you could have a fifth person who assists with processing paperwork behind the scenes while the licensed client service person interacts directly with clients. This additional support is especially important for practices managing over four or five hundred client households.

POSITION #4: RECEPTIONIST

The fourth role is that of a receptionist. This person manages the front desk, greets clients, and ensures smooth daily operations. They make clients feel welcome, engage them in conversation, and offer coffee, especially if the advisor is running late for a meeting. The receptionist also handles incoming phone calls, opens and distributes mail, and performs various clerical tasks. In addition to these duties, the receptionist supports the other three key team members—appointment setter, client service person, and new business processor—with various tasks.

Remember that the receptionist is often the first point of contact for new clients, making their role that much more important. A great receptionist helps maintain your office's professional image and efficient workflow. Not only do they manage appointments, but they also help you operate more seamlessly.

Your First Hire Is the Toughest

Now because it's unlikely you can hire all four positions at once, your first hire is always the toughest because it requires finding someone who can handle a range of responsibilities and adapt.

Assuming you start by hiring a new business processor, you need this person to be left-brained, detail-oriented, and able to manage paperwork without making too many mistakes. You want to avoid NIGOs (not in good order) because they can significantly slow your operations. Instead, this person must have excellent follow-through to ensure nothing falls through the cracks and be capable of filling your calendar by making necessary calls.

Ideally, this first hire will be at least a B player in detail-oriented tasks and people skills, with the potential to become an A player in one area as the practice grows. This part is especially significant because you want to hire people who will grow into the role you envision five years from now. This is why you need to communicate that they will have the opportunity to specialize and "write their own ticket" as the team expands. You will need them to be versatile initially, but over time, they are expected to find one area of one area to excel in.

Once this person is on board, you need to leverage their abilities effectively. If you've never had an assistant before, it's easy to fall into the trap of doing everything yourself. To avoid this, be intentional about delegating tasks. This will free up your time to focus on high-value activities and generate more business. The ultimate goal is to write enough additional business to justify hiring a second person as soon as possible. This approach will help you build a solid foundation for your growing practice.

Your second hire needs to be the opposite of the first. If your first hire was more detail-oriented, you now need someone with more people skills. Appointment setters, for example, tend to be right-brained people who thrive on interaction and sometimes lack the focus on details that the new business processor has. Contrast this with your client service person, who will likely be a blend of both, needing strong people skills combined with some technical acumen.

Now that you have a two-person team, your business will start to take off. You're cooking with oil because you've got a dedicated people person and a detail-oriented person.

The Greatest Hurdle to Building a $50 Million Team

If you're like many advisors I meet, your greatest hurdle in building this $50 million team will be delegation. As an only child, it was easier for me to be a bit selfish and delegate tasks. However, for many, this is a big challenge.

Case in point: several years ago, I was leading a study group at home and had an exchange with one advisor I'll never forget. I was going through the different types of people advisors should have on their teams when I asked everyone in the room this question: "Who's the best in your office at setting appointments?" After going around the circle, each advisor mentioned someone other than themselves, but when I came to a young man named Anthony, an advisor from LA, he kind of shrugged and responded by saying he was.

A few minutes later, I talked about processing new business and asked the same question: "Who's the best in your office at processing new business?" Once again, each advisor listed someone other than themselves, but when it came to Anthony, his response was the same. "That's me!" he said. At this point, everyone started to laugh because it was clear Anthony needed help. He was holding onto everything, thinking he was always the best.

Fast-forward to today, and Anthony has about fifteen people on his team, and he's built a successful organization with several advisors. If you call him now and ask who's responsible for something, he probably won't even know and say something like, "I'm not sure who's in charge of that. Let me talk to Gerry, my operations guy." Anthony used to be a complete control freak, but now he feels liberated because he can focus on growing his business, seeing prospects, and coaching his advisors. When leaders are willing to delegate, their business can grow, but without delegation, everything stagnates.

So let's say you're thinking, *Gee, Dave, delegation is not my problem*. Well, that's good, but there are still gotchas that you need to avoid. Remember earlier that your first hire should be a B player at everything but have the potential to become an A player in one area? My first hire, Suzanne, was great as a one-person team. She was an overall B player who could wear many hats. She was good on the phone, good with people, and efficient with processing business. But when I hired additional staff, she couldn't elevate to being an A player in one specific area and struggled to delegate tasks to the new hires. She was a loyal worker but not suited for a growing team. This experience taught me the importance of hiring people willing to grow with the organization and understand the vision from the start.

Another gotcha to avoid is overworking your first hire and then deciding to hire an assistant for your assistant. This approach is flawed because it forces an assistant, who likely has no management experience, to manage someone else. Instead, it's crucial to allow your team members to specialize in their roles and avoid putting unnecessary managerial pressure on them. Your first hire should be able to grow into their role without managing another person immediately.

This strategy will help you build a more effective and scalable team.

Beware of the Trifecta of Hell

Hiring a team is tough, and delegation is a critical skill. It's common to hear financial advisors say they excel in financial advising and sales but need help with running their businesses. They often lack experience in interviewing and hiring, which leads to poor recruitment decisions.

This brings me to the "trifecta of hell" in hiring financial advisors. First, advisors are salespeople by nature, which makes them susceptible to being sold by a persuasive candidate. Second, hiring an appointment setter or a licensed client service person who is also a salesperson is a recipe for disaster. Third, advisors often want to hire quickly to end the pain of the hiring process, leading to hasty decisions. This results in hiring the wrong person because they lacked a proper hiring process and wanted to stop the misery of interviewing.

Advisors often don't have a structured process for hiring, managing, or holding employees accountable without micromanaging. They might be too lax and have no accountability, leading to situations where important tasks like processing client paperwork are neglected. On the other hand, some advisors micromanage excessively, constantly hovering over their employees, which creates a stifling work environment.

At our companies, we teach advisors to develop healthy hiring processes and effective management techniques that avoid micro-management. If you try to do everything yourself because you're a perfectionist, you'll hit a glass ceiling. Your growth and earnings will be capped, and you'll suffer from burnout. It's death by a thousand paper cuts.

A general rule of thumb is the 80 percent principle.[17] This means that when someone on your team can do something 80 percent as well as you can, it's time to delegate. In time, if they're the right person for the job, their focus on specialization will empower them to exceed you.

---

17   Ilya Pozin, "80% Is Good Enough: Grow Your Business By Delegating," December 17, 2012, https://www.forbes.com/sites/ilyapozin/2012/12/17/80-is-good-enough-grow-your-business-by-delegating/?sh=3ecf847b218c.

Know Where You Want to Go

Ultimately, to grow your business, you must decide if you want to transition from selling to running a business. *Do you have what it takes? What price are you willing to pay?*

Advisors who succeed are humble, coachable, brutally honest with themselves, and continually able to evolve by learning new skills. Not every advisor will make $1,000 an hour—nor should they. But I would encourage you to build your four-person team, focus on what you do best, and delegate the rest.

The key is to reframe the way you think about hiring and your time. Consider this: If hiring someone for $100 an hour (equivalent to $200,000 a year) allows you to make $1,000 an hour, it's a sound investment. While some may balk at the initial cost of bringing someone else on board, if it frees you up to generate ten times your current amount, it's undeniably worth it. Hitting this second level allows you to focus on the most enjoyable and profitable parts of your job while delegating the less valuable tasks. This balance leads to greater job satisfaction and increased income.

In the early 2000s, my four-person team generated $2 million in profit. Even twenty years ago, making $3 million in revenue and netting $2 million after expenses was doable, and now the average size account has tripled, making this much more possible.

But let's say you're not as proficient in sales as Dave Scranton or that work-life balance is more important to you than it was to me. A million-dollar income is now more achievable than ever and more than adequate for a comfortable life. Beyond that, it's about your personal goals and preferences.

For me, mentoring became more fulfilling than seeing clients, so I advanced further. However, if you love prospecting and closing deals, a four-person team can still yield $1 million in annual profits. Many of our advisors achieve this with a four-person team. The key is understanding your strengths and structuring your team to maximize your business enjoyment and income.

But what if you enjoy business growth for the sake of growth or wish to leave a legacy? That's what this next chapter is about.

CHAPTER 7

TURBOCHARGING YOUR BUSINESS

If you've taken the steps described in chapters 1 through 6 and still want more, the last step I'd recommend is to turbocharge your business by building your organization and bringing on other sales advisors.

Maybe you're tired of meeting with clients and prospects and prefer running a business, managing operations, and building something bigger. If so, expanding your team with other financial advisors is a great next step. As I can testify firsthand, it's one of the most rewarding things you can do. This is the $50 million framework on steroids. Here, you're adding client acquisition advisors to your team and taking your business to a much higher level. There are various ways you can do this. You can market through brick-and-mortar offices or decide to have a virtual setup.

You can extend your reach if you opt for a virtual approach—conducting webinars and closing deals through Zoom meetings. But keep in mind the reality is that most salespeople perform better in face-to-face interactions than over Zoom or the telephone. Technology enables us to expand nationally without a physical presence, but face-to-face, knee-to-knee, elbow-to-elbow meetings generally yield better results. Therefore, you must determine how many client acquisition advisors your area can support.

Depending on your local market, you can add more advisors to your primary office, provided you haven't maxed out your ability to market in your geographical location. It all comes down to the number of qualified prospects within driving distance of your office. This will be the limiting factor for the number of advisors you can have in your primary office. Once your base office is at full capacity, setting up satellite offices in strategic locations, like the Edward Jones model, becomes essential.

Five Stages of Entrepreneurial Growth©

To turbocharge your business, you need to identify where you are at and where you want to go. A short time ago, I had my friend Glenn Mattson, from Mattson Enterprise, present at a Sound Income Group event on the Five Stages of Entrepreneurial Growth©. His firm is an office of the Sandler organization, and he has adapted the Sandler philosophy into our world for over the last 30 years. As you review these stages as I interpret them, I'd encourage you to select which stage you are at.

STAGE 1: EMERGING FINANCIAL ADVISOR ENTREPRENEUR

In this initial stage, you are just entering the financial advisory world and face numerous challenges, such as understanding regulations, building your client base, and mastering your services. You may often experience doubt due to inconsistencies in your business efforts, leading to highs and lows in income. This doubt can create immense stress and may be reinforced by significant others. To succeed in this stage, you must quickly learn to sell, grow, and develop mental toughness. You also need to face your fears, take risks, and recover from failures.

STAGE 2: DEVELOPING FINANCIAL ADVISOR ENTREPRENEUR

As a developing financial advisor entrepreneur, you have typically figured out your business model and have a small team of two to four staff members. You succeed in your sales processes and understand your clients' needs and solutions well. However, you may reach a point where you become comfortable with your income level and focus more on maintaining your business rather than growing it. To move to the next level, you must focus on time profitability, delegate tasks, and be willing to invest in your business. You must also avoid treating your business like a hobby and ensure you have proper systems and processes in place.

STAGE 3: RAINMAKER FINANCIAL ADVISOR ENTREPRENEUR

As a rainmaker financial advisor entrepreneur, you are a skilled sales-person who understands the importance of time profitability and often has a larger team. You focus on high-value tasks and delegate lower-value tasks to your staff. You understand the need to invest in your business and measure your return on investment rigorously. You also face the challenge of making critical decisions, often realizing that some long-term team members may not have the skills needed for future growth. You must develop leaders within your team, delegate decision-making, and ensure your business processes are clear and efficient.

STAGE 4: CEO FINANCIAL ADVISOR ENTREPRENEUR

In the CEO stage, you lead the financial advisory business at a strategic level rather than being involved in day-to-day operations. You focus on long-term strategy, looking years ahead rather than months. You have developed your first- and second-line leaders and work on inspiring and guiding your team rather than managing them. You ensure that the business culture and decision-making processes are consistent even when you are not present. You make fewer but more impactful decisions and spend most of your time on strategic initiatives and mentoring your leaders.

STAGE 5: THE MAYOR FINANCIAL ADVISOR ENTREPRENEUR

In the final stage, known as the mayor, you have built a self-sustaining financial advisory business that operates smoothly without your daily involvement. You focus on mentoring, guiding, and developing future leaders within the business. You enjoy seeing others succeed and spend your time on high-level strategy and growth opportunities. This stage is characterized by a significant shift in mindset, where you derive joy from building others and the business itself rather than personal financial gain. You commit deeply to maintaining the values and culture of the business while allowing others to take on leadership roles.

So where are you at in these five stages?

If you're an emerging entrepreneur in the financial advisory field, you should prioritize developing your sales skills, fostering growth, and building mental toughness. It's crucial to face your fears head-on, take calculated risks, and learn to recover from failures quickly. These early steps lay the foundation for your future success.

If you're a developing entrepreneur, focus on maximizing time profitability by delegating tasks effectively and investing wisely in your business. Avoid treating your business like a hobby; instead, establish and adhere to proper systems and processes. This approach ensures sustainable growth and prepares your business for the next stage.

If you're a rainmaker, you must grasp the significance of return on investment (ROI) and delegate decision-making responsibilities to empower your team. Developing leaders within your team is essential, as is making critical decisions about team members to support future growth. This phase involves strategic thinking and effective team management.

If you're a CEO, lead your business strategically, focusing on long-term planning and mentoring leaders. Ensuring consistency in business culture and decision-making processes is vital. Work *on* the business rather than *in* it, guiding its direction and supporting its leaders to drive success.

If you're a mayor, focus on mentoring and guiding future leaders, concentrating on high-level strategy and identifying growth opportunities. Maintain the core values and culture of the business while allowing others to take on leadership roles. This stage is about nurturing the next generation of leaders and ensuring your business's continued prosperity.

**5 Stages of Entrepreneurial Growth©
for Financial Advisors**

Stage 1	Stage 2	Stage 3	Stage 4	Stage 5
Emerging	Developing	Rainmaker	CEO	The Mayor

Moving to Stage 4

Most advisors settle for the first three stages. They want to stop at the rainmaker level as someone who has successfully built a four-person, $50 million team. However, if you desire to go to the fourth stage, and you can allocate a marketing budget, spend money on generating leads, and have someone to book appointments for these prospective advisors, then read on.

As you build your team, you must follow Jim Collins's instructions and get everyone in the right seats on the bus. To do this, you need to understand what motivates each player and what unique skills they possess. Financial advising has three crucial skills: prospecting, converting prospects to clients, and servicing clients to maintain and nurture the relationship. When hiring or assessing advisors, I ask them to rank these skills. Many rank prospecting last and either sales or service first. To test this, I pose a scenario: Imagine one day, you have four meetings with new prospects, and the next day, you have four review meetings with existing clients. Which day leaves you more energized, and which leaves you more tired?

Let's face it: humans don't multitask well. Even when you think you're multitasking, you're really focusing on one thing, quickly switching to the other, and switching back to the former. The reality is that the human brain can only focus on one thing at a time. Thus, when building an organization, it's essential to identify each person's strengths. If advisors focus on their best skills, they will be more energized, perform better, and generate more revenue for both them and the organization.

To optimize this, separate roles into specific departments. Prospectors handle marketing and calls, client acquisition advisors close deals, and service advisors manage client reviews and attempt to garner more assets from existing clients.

Building your team is much like coaching basketball. You need to know who your star players are and the ones who will bring stability. Just as a basketball coach identifies key players for scoring, defense, and leadership on the court, you must recognize which team members excel in driving sales, maintaining client relationships, and ensuring smooth operations. Your star players consistently deliver outstanding results and drive the business forward, while your stable players provide the reliable support and consistency needed for long-term success.

Balancing these roles and understanding each team member's strengths allows you to create a cohesive, high-performing team that can adapt to challenges and seize opportunities. Some financial advisors thrive on the hunt. They love talking with prospects, closing deals, and turning them into clients. However, once the sale is made, they lose interest in servicing the client. They're onto the next "kill" with a hunter mentality. These advisors can make ideal acquisition advisors.

On the other hand, some advisors do better with sales when they have established a long-term relationship. They enjoy nurturing the client relationship and helping clients achieve their financial and investment goals over the years. They seek additional opportunities with existing clients without the stress of converting new prospects into clients. These advisors can make ideal client service advisors.

ADVISOR ROLES

ROLE #1: PROSPECTORS

Prospectors handle the essential tasks of marketing and initiating client contact. They are the first point of engagement, responsible for generating interest and building a pipeline of potential clients. Prospectors ensure a steady flow of scheduled appointments for the organization by focusing on outreach and initial communication, allowing other team members to focus on their specialized tasks. Those that enjoy prospecting the most don't have to be financial advisors. They're essentially the appointment setters we talked about in the previous chapter.

ROLE #2: ACQUISITION ADVISORS

Now when advisors arrive at the office, they already have scheduled appointments ready to go. All they need to do is sit down and meet with prospects with the sole objective of converting them into clients. When it comes to paperwork, such as ACAT paperwork, there's someone available to handle it. As their client base grows, a service person can manage those clients. This setup is ideal for someone who enjoys meeting prospects but lacks the vision or cash flow to build a four-person organization. Their life becomes simpler: they get to make more money than they probably thought possible, and their main focus is converting prospects to clients.

Following your sales process, as discussed in chapter 5, is key. If your advisors adhere to this process, they will convert prospects effectively. Ideally, you should hire people with less than five years of experience because they are more coachable. People with more than five years of experience often have their own established methods and may resist your system.

In my world, if an acquisition advisor meets the minimum performance standards, they earn $165,000 a year, and we are already profitable with that advisor. If they exceed these standards slightly—seeing a few more people, improving their closing ratios, and increasing the average size of their cases—they can make close to $400,000 a year with just average performance. This makes them highly profitable for the organization.

With less than five years of experience, many newer advisors typically earn between $80,000 and $125,000 when they first meet you. However, you can help them earn between $165,000 and $400,000, or more, quickly by providing them with support and a clear path. This substantial investment simplifies their role, allowing them to focus solely on converting prospects to clients. I invest around $200,000 annually in marketing for each acquisition advisor and cover the cost of an appointment set to keep their schedules full.

By offering these resources, they are less likely to leave. Starting independently would require them to lease an office, create a website, learn marketing, manage finances, hire employees, and handle all marketing and lead generation. In contrast, if they can make $165,000 right from the start, more than they ever have before, and potentially up to $400,000 or more after a few years, they will have little incentive to leave. They will make a lot of money and have a true work-life balance.

ROLE #3: SERVICE ADVISORS

While service advisors are not pure hunters, they *can* hunt. They sell better when a client has a relationship with a firm. This position is salaried because they also manage clients who don't present additional sales opportunities. However, they receive bonuses based on how much additional business they bring in from existing clients. It's feasible for a service advisor to earn between $200,000 and $300,000 in total income, making them extremely profitable for the firm. The more experience service advisors have, the better.

Whereas three to five years of experience is optimal for an acquisition advisor, ten to twenty is optimal for a service advisor. If you can hire someone who is a CFP, that's even better. The bottom line is that when the handoff occurs from the acquisition to the service advisor, you don't want new clients to feel like they're being handed down; you want them to feel like they're being handed up to someone with more experience.

While there are some benefits to having nonsolicit agreements, the best way to retain people is by offering so much value that they don't want to leave.

Mistakes to Avoid

That said, how you motivate your team is everything, and you want to keep people with the carrot, not the stick.

One mistake many advisor business owners make is hiring advisors, handing them a phone, and expecting them to make a bunch of calls and bring in clients. They're not getting a lot of value from the business owner, so he or she knows that they'll eventually leave for more services or higher compensation. So the business owner tries to bind these advisors through noncompete or nonsolicit agreements. While there are some benefits to having nonsolicit agreements, the best way to retain people is by offering so much value that they don't want to leave.

You're missing the point if you rely solely on restrictive agreements. In many states, noncompete agreements aren't enforceable, and nonsolicit agreements are starting to lose their teeth. The key is to provide significant value to your advisors.

A second mistake for many business owners in our industry is they fear bringing on other acquisition advisors. The worry is that they're training their future competitors, who will eventually leave. To ease these worries, focus on hiring average salespeople who can stick to a process rather than exceptional salespeople who can't. An average salesperson who follows a process is more likely to succeed. To keep them from leaving, offer enough value to keep them loyal to your organization. Also, you want to look for people who are more team players instead of those who are autonomous. The right kind of testing can help you determine this.

A third critical mistake is allowing the acquisition advisor to service the client, which creates a risk. If the acquisition advisor leaves, they could take their clients with them. To prevent this, I'd recommend that the acquisition advisor hands off the client relationship to a service advisor.

A fourth common mistake I notice is not structuring everyone as W-2 employees. If advisors are 1099 independent contractors, they might not follow your process. By making them W-2 employees, they recognize their role within the company and the necessity to adhere to your processes.

The fifth mistake is not having *all* revenue flow through your office. To prevent side dealings or theft, other firms should not pay your advisors directly. By controlling the revenue stream, you ensure transparency and accountability.

Turbocharging Your Business

Now I don't mean to make this process sound easier than it is. I decided to do it because I realized I was more interested in coaching other advisors than seeing clients.

Building a team is hard work, and I've made many mistakes. Before we started our organization in 2006 and established our Florida headquarters, now known as Sound Income Group, I had a practice in Connecticut. While I was grossing $3 million with $2 million in profit from my production in the early 2000s, I also had eight advisors throughout Connecticut and Rhode Island who were adding to that number.

After 2006, we converted my Connecticut office into a servicing organization with only three employees due to my limited bandwidth. I couldn't build Sound Income Group nationally while managing everything in Connecticut. However, in 2019, I hired a few competent C-suite executives for Sound Income Group to lighten my load.

Simultaneously, some of our top producers, who consistently generated $50 to $100 million in new business annually, approached me. They remembered how I built a large operation with other advisors in the early 2000s and wanted to learn how to do the same. In 2022, I decided to teach them and rebuild what I had in Connecticut. Within two years, we grew from three people to over twenty, including seven acquisition advisors. And it will have grown even more by the time you read this. This success story demonstrates that rapid growth can be achieved by following a proven formula.

Again, our business has a well-defined structure with dedicated roles. We have three people who process new business, three and a half people who are appointment setters keeping calendars filled, and seven acquisition advisors. Only two of our acquisition advisors are based in our home office; the rest operate out of branch offices due to the limited population near our home office. Additionally, we have three service advisors. This setup ensures that everyone focuses on their niche.

Life is good. However, I want to overemphasize that I'm not trying to force you into a shoe that doesn't fit. You don't have to grow to seven advisors; you can stop at two, three, or four or expand to ten or fifteen. There's no limit. Once you learn the formula, you can replicate it in another geographical area. The key is to know what's right for you and to motivate others by the carrot and not the stick.

While it might take a while to get to where you want to go, I hope you carefully note these steps I've outlined and develop the right philosophy and practices for your business. Gradually, as you make good decisions day after day, these will compound to turbocharge you, your team, and your business.

CHAPTER 8

THE POWER OF SENSORY-SPECIFIC GOALS

To become an attraction-based financial advisor who develops a team and leads a thriving business, you must set clear and compelling goals.

Unfortunately, many people think of goals as token objectives they write down on paper but have yet to achieve. They're nice ideas but unlikely to become reality. Case in point: Before I became independent, I was an advisor at a mutual insurance company in the mid-'80s. My manager would come to me there and ask what my goals were from year to year. Not wanting to upset him, I would give him a number I thought he wanted to hear.

I'd say something like, "I want to make $200,000 next year," and he'd walk away happy with my aspirations and share these with his manager. It didn't matter to him that I never hit these goals. All that was important was that I had them. This established a bad pattern in my life because I lost confidence in my ability after not achieving my goals for several years.

It wasn't until I had that moment I referenced in chapter 6, when I found myself sitting on a beach on Nantucket Island and setting my goal to earn $1,000 an hour, that things changed. I knew the only way I would achieve what Jim Collins called a BHAG (big hairy audacious goal) was to have a big hairy audacious plan! This realization made me confront my limiting beliefs, acknowledging that I needed to change.

But as you may recall from earlier in the book, by 1995, I had worked as a struggling financial advisor for eight years. This was the point I contemplated leaving the business to fulfill my childhood aspiration of becoming a doctor. But again, as I shared earlier, I knew I could not leave as a failure. So this was when I set my goal to earn $125,000 in 1996. I had no clue how to achieve the goal, except I found a mentor, worked super hard, and earned $127,000 that year. I woke up on January 1, 1997, wondering if it was a fluke or if I could do it again. I set a goal to make $175,000 that year, got focused, worked hard, and earned $183,000. After two years of success, my lack of belief in my ability to set and achieve goals turned into complete confidence that I could do it.

Part of my success in achieving my goals in 1996 and 1997 was because of the sensory-specific goals I'd set a few years earlier on Nantucket Island. It triggered the part of my mind known as the reticular activating system, which allowed me not only to notice opportunities that could help me reach my goals but also motivate me to do so. When you have goals that truly inspire you, your sub-conscious mind notices and seizes opportunities that might have otherwise been overlooked.

It's like when you buy a red sports car—suddenly, you start seeing that car everywhere. This happens because your subconscious mind is now attuned to it. The same principle applies to business goals. When you write your goals in sensory-specific detail, you program your sub-conscious mind to spot opportunities that align with your goals. After achieving my goals in 1996 and 1997, my confidence soared, and I realized I could set and achieve any goal I wanted.

With my reticular activating system in full gear, I noticed opportunities everywhere. In eight years, I had lost confidence in my ability to achieve goals, but in just two years, I regained it completely. I write this because, regardless of whether you're having a record year or a challenging one, setting your goals in writing is crucial because the past does not equal the future.

How to Set Goals That Stick

The problem is that most of us were taught to think about goals the wrong way. For example, let's say you have a goal to make $500,000 a year. How will you get to $500,000? To achieve this, most goal-setting frameworks suggest you start by figuring out how many closes you need based on your average case size. Then you determine how many first appointments you need to reach that number of closes, followed by how many leads you need to generate those first appointments. Finally, you backtrack to see how much marketing is required to get those leads. This is all essential for mapping out how to achieve your $500,000 goal.

However, this is only the second half of the goal-setting process. The first part concerns motivation and inspiration. What makes this goal worth achieving? Most people are motivated by something other than the $500,000 number. In their minds, it is just a five followed by five zeros with a comma in between.

While you might think earning $500,000 a year will make you feel successful, and that's motivation enough, I respectfully disagree. For most people, money is nothing more than green pieces of paper with the faces of dead presidents printed on one side. What truly motivates people is knowing everything $500,000 can do for them and their families. This is where a good sensory-specific goal-setting process can help.

Think about everything you want to have, do, or become—financially, in relationships, fitness, spirituality, and achievements—so you can understand what earning $500,000 will truly mean to you. Again, this represents the first half of a good goal-setting process.

These are all aspects you want to focus on in your goals and everything you want to have, do, or become in each category. It's not enough to write down, "I want to have a net worth of $5 million," "I want to be a good husband and father," "I want to be fit," "I want to have a great relationship with my higher power," or "I want to buy a beach home and a nice car." The key to achieving these goals is to engage your subconscious mind.

While modern psychological science disputes the claim that we only use 10 percent of our brainpower,[18] I think it's safe to say most humans don't always fire on all cylinders. We fill our minds with junk or meaningless entertainment and don't engage with those things that matter most. However, when we set sensory-specific goals, everything changes. These engage every part of our being. This is why I always encourage people I mentor to set their goals in a way that allows them to see, hear, smell, feel, and taste them.

People who excel at setting and achieving goals have one thing in common: they vividly imagine living their goal long before they achieve it. By the time they actually reach their goal, it feels almost anticlimactic because they have already experienced it so many times in their minds.

---

18   Stephen L. Chew, "Myth: We Only Use 10% of Our Brains," Association for Psychological Science, August 29, 2018, https://www.psychologicalscience.org/uncategorized/myth-we-only-use-10-of-our-brains.html.

Keep Chasing

Around 2006, before we started Advisors' Academy, I bought a seventy-five-foot motor yacht that I had for four years. One night, one of my best friends sat with me on the bridge. It was my first night enjoying this new boat with friends, and as I stared off into space, my friend said, "I bet I know what you're thinking about." I turned and laughed, asking, "Well, what is it?" He replied, "You're thinking about your next goal." I laughed again and said, "You know what? Darn it, you're right. That's exactly what I was thinking."

> You can enjoy what you have and still pursue the next thing.

Now some of you might read this and say, "Hey, live in the present. Enjoy what you have. You just got the new boat and are already thinking about the next goal. What are you chasing?" The truth is, you can enjoy what you have and still pursue the next thing. It's not an either-or situation.

When you set goals that genuinely motivate you, achieving the goal isn't the ultimate reward. It's about the journey to the goal. The process of moving from point A to point B is what you find enjoyable. I planned to enjoy that boat for many years, and I did. But once I set that goal, the actual achievement was somewhat of a letdown. Why? Because, in my mind, I had mastered the art of living that goal in a sensory-specific fashion long before I bought the boat.

Whenever I set a short-term goal, achieve it, and buy or do something I want, I often experience a lull in energy and focus afterward. Why? Because I haven't set my next goal yet. To maintain momentum, you need to set new goals continuously. Your goals encompass everything you want to have, do, or become in several areas.

When I purchased that boat, I felt I had already achieved it. Thus, the act of buying the boat was anticlimactic; it just meant writing a check. But in my mind, I had vividly lived that experience many times over the years. So once the excitement of the purchase was over, I enjoyed the boat, but I was ready for the next chase.

And here is what was kind of funny. Before purchasing this yacht, I had been on probably over twenty similar yachts. The company that made them only made around forty of them, and I had been on nearly half. I knew every nook and cranny of that boat so well that the first night I slept on it, I had an unusual experience.

Normally, when you wake up in a new place in the dark, you must feel your way around to find the bathroom. But I got up, confidently walked to the bathroom, turned on the light, did my business, turned off the light, and went back to bed without hesitation. It was only the next morning that I realized what I had done. Being that comfortable in a new place on the first night is so rare. Why? Because I had been on more than twenty such boats and knew every detail. I had already lived that dream in my mind.

Control What You Visualize

Some of us, however, don't realize we can control what we visualize. Think about people who suffer from anxiety—they often have a negative playlist playing in their minds. Those who worry excessively typically think about the worst-case scenarios. This negative loop plays continuously, causing anxiety because they feel a lack of control.

The good news is that you can control your mind and focus on your thoughts. By learning to set your goals in a sensory-specific way, you can remove that negative playlist, delete it, and replace it with a positive one that aligns with your goals. So when you're anxious or worried, you can switch out the negative playlist for a positive one, visualizing yourself achieving your goals. The human mind has an incredible capacity to dream and visualize, allowing you to imagine living your goals long before they happen.

This ability to change your mental state is powerful. You can shift from a negative, worried state to a confident, empowered one instantly by changing the playlist in your mind. The key is to have a library full of these positive playlists—goals, aspirations, and everything you want to have, do, or become. With this library ready, you can quickly swap out a negative playlist for a positive one, transforming your state from worrisome and negative to empowering and positive.

Build Momentum and Set Sensory-Specific Goals

As you do this, you will build momentum. Momentum is a force to be reckoned with, whether you're riding the wave or getting crushed by it. If you've ever been caught in an undertow, you know how powerful it can be. So keep that momentum going. If you're having a record year, maintain it. I encourage you to set your goals for next year, stretch your comfort zone, challenge yourself, and put your business plan together.

Maybe you haven't had a record year. This can be discouraging, leading you to stop setting goals altogether. If that's the case, remember that the past doesn't equal the future. Just because you haven't achieved your goals in the past doesn't mean you won't achieve them in the future.

Again, it's not just about financial goals. It's about setting goals that engage your subconscious mind and reticular activating system. How do you do that? The most important thing is to allow yourself to dream. When you were young, you weren't afraid to dream big. You'd say, "I want to be a fireman" and "I want to be a millionaire" in the same breath. Children don't worry about practicality; they just dream. Only as they grow older do they learn to be "practical," and their dreams get smaller and smaller.

However, to set sensory-specific goals, you must think big and dream like a child. Go somewhere that motivates you, away from the office, your spouse, and the kids. Shut off your phone, sit with a pad of paper, and engage in stream-of-consciousness writing. Write about everything you want in your life. Initially, it will be slow because your adult mind will resist, saying, "That's too big, too ridiculous." But once you quiet that voice and allow yourself to dream, the ideas flow more easily.

Create "Have," "Do," and "Become" Goals

Write everything you've ever wanted to have, do, or become. Then break each one down and write about them in sensory-specific detail using all six senses. For example, instead of just writing "I want a beach home," describe what it would be like to lie in bed with the window open, hearing the waves crash, smelling the salt air, waking up and walking on the beach with a cup of coffee, feeling the sand between your toes and the sun on your skin. Engage all your senses in your writing to create a vivid mental image.

The "have" goals are easy. When you start working in financial sales, if you want to buy a certain type of car, they tell you to take a picture of that car and pin it to your wall as a constant visual reminder of the car. These are easy. For example, I know one advisor who wrote a detailed vision of his dream house, including the foyer, living room, kitchen, and more. Years later, he had that house built and paid for in cash. Why? Because he had a clear, sensory-specific image of what he wanted.

The "do" goals and "become" goals are more difficult because they require more creativity to write about them in a sensory-specific fashion. I think of one advisor who had a goal to spend one month each year in Africa on a mission. To get there, he wrote a detailed story about what this would look like, focusing on the experience and the emotions of helping children in need. This spiritual goal motivated him to work toward his financial goals.

Another advisor wanted to take his whole family to Italy. So he wrote about his experience in detail, from the exhaustion of the red-eye flight to the smells and sounds of the cafes. This vivid imagery motivated him to achieve his goal and take his family on that trip.

One of the most powerful ways to create "do" goals is to imagine what life would be like for those you loved if you achieved them. Imagine how it would feel to tell your daughter that she can attend the college of her choice because you hit your financial goals. Contrast that with the feeling of having to tell her she must go to a state school regardless of her qualifications because you didn't meet your goals and can't afford anything else. Again, you need to write about these scenarios in sensory-specific detail.

"Become" goals can be the most challenging to explore in a sensory-specific fashion. Here is the key: before considering dollar amounts, reflect on everything you want to become regarding relationships, fitness, and spiritual achievements.

Think about how great it feels to have date nights and a relationship with your spouse just as strong twenty-five or thirty years into the marriage as it was in the first five years. Write about this in sensory-specific language—how it looks, sounds, and feels. The same goes for all relationships. Consider fitness: what it feels like to run down the beach with your grandchildren without getting winded, feeling fit and confident. Write about it vividly. Spirituality is similar. Envision your spiritual life and why it's important to you. Describe it in all its sensory details.

Setting goals to achieve can also be a powerful motivator. For example, I know one advisor who always wanted a PhD. He dreamt about being greeted in a restaurant with "Welcome, Dr. and Mrs. Jones. Let me show you to your table." That motivated him. While this goal might not motivate others, it worked for him, and now he has his PhD.

It's crucial to figure out what motivates *you* and write about it. If your motivation is for the greater good, write in a sensory-specific way about how you can help people and what that means to you. One useful exercise is to write your own eulogy. Imagine what people would say about you after you die. If you're motivated by helping others, consider how good it would feel to be remembered positively, like the Mother Teresa of the financial world.

Do Something

I know my goal-setting process is complex. If you want to take a shortcut, perhaps you could follow Brian Tracy's advice and write down your top ten goals from memory every day. You can't cheat because if you forget a goal or it gets replaced by something else, that's okay. If you forget a goal, it isn't that important to you. But just by writing them down every day, you'll keep your reticular activating system, your subconscious mind, firing on all cylinders.

However, when I tell you to go through my complete process, it's not because I want you to waste an entire day. It's because I know it works. Writing down your goals is good but setting them in writing in a sensory-specific fashion is far more effective.

This approach allowed me to bring in over $60 million in new assets annually in the early 2000s by working with average folks. And I'm sure the numbers would have been much larger if I had more affluent clients. I know what motivates me, and our advisors who exceed their goals by a large margin know what motivates them too. Regardless of where you're at, you need to figure out what you want in your life and

> If you don't know what motivates you, you owe it to yourself, your family, and your clients to figure it out.

then determine how much income you need to achieve it. Then you can start traditional goal setting. Starting with the income amount alone won't motivate you. Figuring out your true motivations will.

If you don't know what motivates you, you owe it to yourself, your family, and your clients to figure it out. Motivation should have a couple of prongs. One is personal goals, and the other is helping people. Let's face it: we're in a heap of trouble as a nation, and people are scared about the future. This means if you're motivated by helping people, now is the best time to be an advisor. Now is the time to act and make a difference.

Explore Your Ideal Day in the Office

A final exercise I recommend is writing about your ideal day at the office. Describe your perfect day, including what you do and how you feel. Remember that story I shared about when I sat on that beach on Nantucket Island and wrote down my goals? I can't stress how significant this moment was, so it's worth repeating.

After repeatedly hitting obstacles, I decided to take a few days off to set some goals. My place of choice was Nantucket Island in the northeast, where I spent seventy-two hours in the middle of summer sitting at the end of a beach, working on my goals. Reflecting on a statistic I'd heard in the early '90s, I realized that an advisor's face-to-face time with a qualified prospect could be worth $500 to $1,000 an hour, translating to $1 to $2 million a year if done forty hours a week.

I questioned why I was earning a fraction of that and recognized that I needed to spend more time in front of prospects. Instead, I was bogged down with other duties. This stemmed from my limiting beliefs, thinking only I could handle tasks like calling referrals and client services. However, sitting on that beach, I knew something needed to change. To become an advisor worth $1,000 an hour, I realized I needed to create a team of four people and refocus my efforts on high-value work.

This exercise helped me identify what truly mattered most. I visualized my ideal day, and now I live it, focusing on high-value tasks and delegating the rest. I attribute every goal I've achieved since 1996 to when I sat on that beach on Nantucket Island and wrote down my goal to create a four-person team. As I did this, I wasn't just creating the perfect future but the perfect *day*. Now I get to be one of those rare individuals who says they never work a day in their lives. While some days are tougher than others, I genuinely love going to work each day. I'm doing the stuff I'm great at and delegating the rest.

As I wrap up this book, I challenge you to have your own Nantucket experience. Find a place to get away and write your goals in sensory-specific detail. Visualize what a perfect day at the office might look like. Then establish a clear plan to get you where you need to be. Bring alongside mentors who can help you and force yourself to delegate tasks others can do.

When you set goals, the key is knowing where you want to go so you can create a road map to get there. Balance your short-term and long-term goals. Setting goals is essential whether you had a terrible year or a record year. Remember, the past does not equal the future.

With a little hard work, clear goals, and proper focus, you can create the life and business you've only dreamed is possible.

CONCLUSION

And just like that, we've reached the end!

To recap, the foundation of this book starts by following the AIDA outline. This path from chasing to attracting clients is not just a change in strategy; it's a shift in mindset. This mindset starts with generating *attention*. By differentiating yourself from the competition, you become a magnet for prospects. Sparking *interest* involves communicating your unique value proposition effectively. Once interest is piqued, the goal is to create *desire*. This is where lead generation comes into play. Finally, turning desire into *action* means closing the deal. This involves guiding your prospects through a clear process that highlights the value you bring.

As I've shared, these principles have been the foundation of my success, and I wrote this book to share the hard-earned lessons and strategies that have worked for me and the countless other advisors I've mentored. My hope is that you can apply these insights to accelerate your own path to success. Who knows? Maybe you'll be one of the success stories I reference in my next book!

However, keep in mind that success doesn't stop at attracting and converting clients. This is why you must set clear, sensory-specific goals and develop your $50 million team. Only as you take these steps can you turbocharge your business.

As you apply the principles and strategies this book outlines, remember that the journey is ongoing. Continuous learning and adaptation are key to staying relevant and successful. So embrace the challenges, celebrate your victories, and strive for excellence.

If you want to know more about how Sound Income Group can help you attract and not chase, visit our website (www.soundincomegroup.com) or call our office (800-768-6333) and ask for one of our business development specialists.

ACKNOWLEDGMENTS

After you've spent over thirty years building a successful career that has included writing three previous books, acknowledging those who have helped you along the way becomes increasingly challenging. Not because you've already publicly acknowledged them all in the past, but because the list keeps growing! Any measure of forward progress in life or business depends on finding and surrounding yourself with the right people. There will be missteps from time to time. Poor fits. But the "good fits" are essential to your own increasing growth and success; the more you grow, the more of them you need to find.

My "good fits" already know how much they're appreciated, and many of them have already been acknowledged in previous books. These include my long-time loyal clients, of course, as well as the core group of financial advisors who have been with me since I first launched Advisors' Academy (now Sound Income Academy). Although I have ostensibly always been their coach, I have learned as much from them over the years as they have from me.

The "good fits" I would like to newly acknowledge in this book are the many hardworking team members who have helped me build and grow Sound Income Group and its affiliate companies: Sound Income Strategies, Sound Income Academy, and Retirement Income

Source®, as well as my personal practice in Connecticut, Scranton Financial Group.

This large and incredibly talented group of professionals has been—and continues to be—essential to my ability to successfully achieve my mission in life. That mission, simply put, is to teach hard-working Americans all over the country that they can get more income from their investments with less risk of spending down principal, and thereby enjoy a better, happier retirement.

Although there are too many of them to name individually, every team member in each of these companies is a vital contributor to my mission. Without their efforts, my vision could never have become a reality, and its continued growth and success would not be possible. I am grateful to all for their important contributions!

ABOUT THE AUTHOR

David J. Scranton CFA®, CFP®, ChFC®, CLU®, is a nationally known money manager and the founder of Sound Income Group, Sound Income Strategies, Retirement Income Source®, and Sound Income Academy. He is recognized as one of the industry's leading business mentors, sales coaches, and authorities on investing for income. He has made a name for himself by helping investors nationwide achieve their retirement goals and by teaching hundreds of fellow advisors how to do likewise while achieving dramatic business growth in the process.

David's prosperity is a product of the achievements of the many advisors he has coached and mentored. Likewise, the success of those advisors stems from their ability to provide clients with reliable investment alternatives aligned with their goals and actively managed through Sound Income Strategies, Dave's SEC Registered Investment Advisory and money management firm.

David has frequently shared his market insights on networks such as Fox Business, CNBC, and Bloomberg. He also has his own radio show, "The Retirement Income Source," and hosts the popular "Retirement Income Source" YouTube channel. For four years David hosted the nationally televised program "The Income Generation" on which he discussed the markets and investing with some of the most renowned thought leaders in the industry, including Steve Forbes,

Robert Shiller, Marc Faber, and Peter Schiff. David's books include the Amazon bestsellers *Retirement Income Source: The Ultimate Guide to Eternal Income* and *Return on Principle: 7 Core Values to Help Protect Your Money in Good Times and Bad.*

CONTACT PAGE

Sound Income Group

500 West Cypress Creek Road, Suite 250

Fort Lauderdale, FL, 33309

800-768-6333

800-SOUND-33

contact@soundincomegroup.com